MARRIAGE
BY THE BOOK

MARRIAGE

BY THE

BOOK

Rick and Rebekah Porterfield

Printed in the United States of America

ISBN: 978-0-9816532-2-8

CONTENTS

DEDICATION

We dedicate this book to our children,
Vincent, Sidney, Spenser and Madison

ACKNOWLEDGEMENTS

We want to give a big thank you to our parents, Gary and Sandi Bader and Lee and Charlotte Porterfield, for all of their love, support, and encouragement through the years.

INTRODUCTION

Read This First

THIS is a book about how to make good marriages better, how to make bad marriages good, and how to breathe life into dead marriages. It's about succeeding even when the whole world says you have lost. We can assure you from personal experience that no matter how bad your marriage is it can be saved, and no matter how good your marriage is, it can be made better.

We went from a marriage that was about as bad as you can possibly imagine to a great marriage. How bad was our marriage? A Ph.D. psychologist we were seeing for counseling told us that we were the only hopeless case she had ever seen, and that we should get a divorce. That's pretty bad. A recommendation like that from an "expert" leaves little hope. But God brought our marriage back from the dead and He will do the same for you. The last chapter in this book gives our testimony in detail. We included it so that others can see that it is possible to save even the worst of marriages.

Even if your marriage is good, the principles in this book can help make it even better. These are the things you should be doing no matter where you are in your relationship.

God created marriage; He knows better than anyone how to have good relationships. He knows how to give you a great marriage. I like the way Jeremiah 29:11 reads in The Message Bible,

"I know what I'm doing. I have it all planned out--plans to take care of you, not abandon you, plans to give you the future you hope for."

That is God talking to you!

In marriage two people become one. Imagine water and oil mixed together in a small bottle. These are two very different substances. To mix them, to make them one, you have to really shake that little bottle. As soon as you stop shaking, the two will begin to separate. It takes effort and work to make them one and keep them that way. Quit making an effort, and these two different substances will quite naturally, and without any effort on your part, begin to separate. If the two were well mixed to start with, it might take a while for the separation to even become noticeable. It might be so gradual that you just won't notice it for a while, but it will happen. Marriage is like this. You and your spouse are different. You have to work at it for the two of you to become one; stop working, and with no effort on your part, the two of you will drift apart. All you have to do to have separation in your marriage is nothing.

This book is about making two people one and keeping them that way.

While working to improve your marriage, it is important to keep your focus on you. It is very easy to think, "My spouse needs to do this or that" or "My spouse needs to be the one reading this book." The reality is that you can't make your spouse do anything. Keep the focus on you. What should you be doing? How should you be reacting? You do your part.

I want to say one final thing in introducing this book. Everybody has problems in marriage. Nobody is exempt. Some have more, some have less, but everybody has some. The devil lies to people by saying that they are the only ones who have any problems. We hear the lie, believe it, and think that something is wrong with us. It makes us afraid to get help. "What if I tell someone and they laugh at me or ostracize me or look down on me. I can't tell anyone." So, we suffer in silence, but you don't need to; this is, after all, just a lie. We all deal with the same stuff to one extent or another. Scripture bears this out.

1 Peter 5:9 (NKJV)
"Resist him, steadfast in the faith, knowing that the same sufferings are experienced by your brotherhood in the world."

1 Corinthians 7:28 (NKJV)
"But even if you do marry, you have not sinned; and if a virgin marries, she has not sinned. Nevertheless such will have trouble in the flesh, but I would spare you."

You see, even God says that we are all dealing with the same types of problems, and He specifically says that married people will experience troubles. So, there is nothing wrong with you. You aren't weird. It is normal. The thing you need to do is learn how to handle what is going on.

This book will help you do that.

Chapter 1

THE PROBLEM
IN RELATIONSHIPS

WHEN you get down to it, there is just one root problem in relationships. All other problems are just symptoms of this root problem. Rebekah and I call it "THE" problem. This one thing can take any situation, big or small, and turn it into a major relationship battle.

Maybe you are thinking, "This is silly. There is more than one problem in marriage relationships. People fight about all kinds of things."

This is very true. But again, one root problem is the cause of all those other problems. For example, have you ever had the flu? Most everyone has had it. As you know, it can cause lots of nasty symptoms like fever, headache, tiredness, cough, sore throat, stuffiness, body and muscle aches, runny nose, wheezing, chills, loss of appetite, vomiting, and dizziness. All of these different symptoms are caused by the one root problem—the flu virus— operating in your body. You can take flu medicine and get rid of the symptoms for a little while, but until the flu virus itself is gone, the symptoms will return.

In the same way, all of the problems you encounter in a marriage relationship are caused by the one true root problem. People fight about all kinds of issues, money, kids, sex, communication, priorities, and even trivial things like what kind of toothpaste you use or about leaving the toilet seat up or down. Every argument you have about anything is simply a symptom of the true problem. Until the root problem is addressed, the symptoms will keep coming back.

Early in our marriage, when Rebekah and I would have an argument over one of these symptoms, I would be very careful for a while not to do it again. But inevitably, in a few weeks or a few months we would be having the same argument all over again because I had committed the same offense. The reason was because we were trying to treat the symptoms of the problem and not the problem itself. Treating the symptoms is just a short-term fix. If the problem is taken care of, the symptoms will take care of themselves.

So what is THE PROBLEM?

What is the problem? What causes us to have all of these arguments? The answer may surprise you.

Here is how I found out what "THE" problem is. I was sitting in my bedroom one day, after Rebekah and I had gotten into one of those recurring arguments, praying and agonizing over these very questions. This was in 1994. I just knew deep inside that there had to be some root problem; a "bottom line" cause. I just sensed it. I had heard various ministers and other experts try to answer this question of what was "THE" problem in marriage relationships. The most common answer I had heard was that lack of communication was the problem. Another answer I had heard was having your priorities out of order is the problem. Other possible answers I had heard included money, sex, kids, and so on.

None of these possible answers seemed quite right. They just didn't hit it on the head. For example, I could communicate and communicate and communicate and still have problems in my marriage. In fact, if I talked too much, I could make things worse. Also, no matter how much money you have there can be arguments about how to spend it or whether to save it. So, there in my bedroom, I asked God, "Father, what is the root cause of offenses in marriage relationships? Why do the same problems keep coming up over and over again?" I was amazed when God answered me, but His answer was not at all what I expected! He said very clearly, "Self-centeredness is the problem." Now don't try to tell me I imagined that! I was amazed to think that me being self-centered was the problem in my marriage; Rebekah just had to be responsible is some way, didn't she? Probably the last thing I would ever have imagined was that my being self-centered was the problem. It was definitely God I heard.

The best way I can describe my reaction to this answer is that it was like a flower blooming in my head. From this one word of knowledge sprang a great wealth of understanding. I suddenly saw clearly that the root problem in marriage is that we each tend to put our own needs, wants, and desires, over the needs, wants, and desires of our spouse. The same can also be said for relationships in general - the problem in relationships is that we all tend to put ourselves first and others, including God, second.

Now, this is far too important a point for me to expect you to just take my word for it. In fact, I told God, "Lord, no one is going to believe me. You need to show me this in the Bible." He did show it to me. It is found in the scripture shown below.

James 4:1(CEV)
"Why do you fight and argue with each other? "Isn't it because you are full of selfish desires that fight to control your body?"

Here we see James asking the same question I asked in the bedroom that day, and he gets the same answer. He says the cause is our selfish desires. Plainly, the Bible confirms that conflicts in relationships are caused by our tendency to put ourselves first. This is nothing more than self-centeredness.

Maybe you are thinking, "Okay, that's just one scripture. Is that all you've got?" Actually, no. Scriptures can be found all over the Bible that point to the same thing. Here are a couple of them:

Galatians 6:8 (CEV)
"If you follow your selfish desires, you will harvest destruction, but if you follow the Spirit, you will harvest eternal life."

James 1:14 (NKJV)
"But each one is tempted when he is drawn away by his own desires and enticed."

We will be looking at more scriptures on the subject as we go along.

Self-centeredness can be defined as being concerned with our own desires, needs, interests, pleasures, or advantage without regard to others. To have a good marriage, we need to be other-centered. Being other-centered means that we give no thought to ourselves and we put others above us on our priority list.

Self-centeredness is without a doubt the problem in relationships. In this chapter we will discuss all of the effects of self-centeredness including the magnitude of this problem, its dangers, its deceptiveness, and the burden it creates. Full knowledge of this problem will help you get victory over it—remember, God said, "my people are destroyed for lack of knowledge" (Hosea 4:6, NKJV).

The Effects of The Problem

Self-centeredness has many effects on relationships. It destroys relationships. It destroys success in your life. It leads to manipulation. It creates symptoms in your relationship. It steals your joy and happiness. It causes unintentional offenses. Let's look at each of these in a little more detail.

Destroys Relationships

Self-centeredness destroys relationships. Not only does it destroy your relationship with your spouse, it also can destroy your relationship with God, your children, parents, in-laws, friends, and your pastor. It even destroys relationships between nations and races. Self-centeredness impacts relationships in all of these situations. But I believe that self-centeredness is more likely to cause big problems in the marriage relationship than in any other relationship. This happens because you are with your spouse for longer periods of time than you are with anyone else, and you are with them in so many different situations. Who else sees you when you go to bed and when you get up; when you are tired and when you are rested; when you are unshaved or don't have your makeup on? Your spouse sees you at your best and at your worst. You can't fool them for long. If you are looking out for your own interests, you'll run into trouble when your interests don't agree with those of your spouse. One or possibly both of you could be inconvenienced and offended. This results in damage to your relationship.

For example, suppose you are going out one night to eat. You want Mexican and your spouse wants Chinese; your interests have just crossed your spouse's and tension may result from trying to decide where to eat (unless you happen to have a Chinese-Mexican place in your town). If you insist on your way and your spouse insists on their way, conflict will result. Someone, preferably both, needs to be other-centered to avoid trouble.

Destroys Success

Self-centeredness will destroy success in your life. In the book, *How to Win Friends and Influence People*, Dale Carnegie cites a study done in the 1930s by the Carnegie Institute of Technology. This study showed that 15% of a person's success in life is based on technical ability, and 85% is based on your ability to deal with and get along with people. John Maxwell, in *The Winning Attitude*, cites a similar study conducted not so many years ago by the Stanford Research Institute. This study showed that the money you will make in any endeavor is based 12.5% on your technical ability and 87.5% on your ability to deal with people. We have already established that self-centeredness is the problem in relationships; based on this research it is obvious that self-centered people will tend to be less successful than those who put other's needs, wants and desires first.

The importance that "playing nice" has on your success in life may come as a surprise to some people. Maybe it shouldn't since the Bible says the same thing. Take a look at this.

1 Corinthians 6:12 (AMP)
"Everything is permissible (allowable and lawful) for me; but not all things are helpful (good for me to do, expedient and profitable when considered with other things). Everything is lawful for me, but I will not become the slave of anything or be brought under its power."

The Message Bible renders the last part of this scripture as being, *"... a slave to my whims."* Even though you are free and can do what you want, you would be foolish to become a slave to your own whims. That is the "broad way" that Jesus talks about in Matthew Chapter 7, and it leads to destruction. Think about it. You are free to run headfirst into a tree if you want to, but is that profitable? No! At the very least you'll get a big knot on your head and maybe worse. Likewise, you are free to be self-centered, but is that profitable? Both the Bible, and the studies cited above agree it is not.

Successful businesses learned long ago that they must be other-centered to build a good relationship with customers. "The customer is always right" is an often quoted business axiom. To maximize success, a company must put the wants, needs, and interests of its customers first. Not doing so will likely mean declining profits and eventually business failure. Major corporations spend millions of dollars every year on market research to find out how people like their products, what changes or improvements they would like to see made to the products, and what new products they may want.

For example, back in the mid-1980s the folks at Coca Cola decided to change their formula. It was a disaster. People hated the new sweeter Coke and wanted the old Coke back. Coca Cola failed to be other-centered when they introduced the new Coke, but they didn't blow it twice. They quickly put their old drink back on the market under the name Coca Cola Classic. Companies have much greater success when they put their customers first. Your marriage will not succeed unless you put your spouse above yourself. The last part of Galatians 5:13 bears this out. It says "...*through love you should serve one another.*"

Leads to Manipulation

Self-centeredness can also lead you to manipulate your spouse. Here is why. When people get married even though they are in love, usually they think the person they are marrying will meet their needs and make them happy. They are looking for such things as companionship, love, security, sex, someone to make the money, someone to do the laundry—the list is endless! They expect to get these things from the person they are marrying. Think about it—this is a totally self-centered attitude. Yet, it is probably the norm for most people. They get married to receive, not to give.

How often do you see someone get married intending to put themselves second, and having the attitude that they will try to meet the needs of their spouse whether or not their own needs get met? This almost never happens, but this is the other-centered attitude you should have. What really happens, however, is you expect to receive. When you don't get what you want, you begin trying to manipulate your spouse through your words and actions (whining, complaining, grouching, cold shoulder, etc.) to get them to give you what you want. Manipulation of your spouse can never lead to intimacy and a good marriage. In fact, manipulation is the direct opposite of serving or ministering to someone.

Creates Symptoms

Another effect of self-centeredness is it creates symptoms in relationships. All of the offenses, the common reasons for arguing, that we talked about at the beginning of this chapter are symptoms of the real problem which is self-centeredness. Symptoms can include things like fights over sex, money, kids, communication, time, leaving the toilet seat up or down, where to go on vacation, putting your socks in front of the clothes hamper instead of in it, baking the chicken instead of frying it, and so on. These are just a few of the infinite number of symptoms that self-centeredness can cause. All of the little problems in your marriage that irritate you are just symptoms. All of the big problems in your marriage that you think you can't get over are symptoms.

When Rebekah and I used to talk about the things that were wrong in our marriage, we would list all of these things (not realizing they were just symptoms) and say, "If you just wouldn't do these things, we would have a much better marriage." Rebekah could usually list many more things about me than I could list about her. She would list things like stop lying, stop getting drunk, stop working all the time, stop wearing earplugs when you are at home. She had some good ones.

I used to tell her that all of these things were like a giant swarm of gnats and there was no way I could swat them all. I felt like there were just too many, and no matter what I did they just kept coming. I was right. The "gnats" were symptoms and there was no way to swat them all. As long as their source remained, they just kept coming. You cannot get rid of all the irritations in marriage as long as the source, self-centeredness, remains.

Steals Joy and Happiness

The next effect of self-centeredness that I want to discuss is that it steals your joy and happiness. Self-centered people expect others to meet their needs and make them happy. They are like a drug addict looking for a fix. When the high of one fix wears off, the good feeling is gone, and they are looking for the next fix. When we rely on others to make us happy, we are doing the same thing. The temporary high wears off, and we expect someone else, usually our spouse, to make us happy again. Consider the following scripture.

1 Timothy 5:6 (AMP)
"Whereas she who lives in pleasure and self-gratification [giving herself up to luxury and self-indulgence] is dead even while she [still] lives."

Selfish people are dead even while they live. That doesn't sound like much fun does it? In the long run, there is just no pleasure in serving yourself. The only way to find happiness is to do things God's way and serve others. We will talk more about that later. Note this scripture is specifically referring to a woman, but the same is true for men; the gender in this scripture is not the key—the selfish attitude is.

Unintentional Offenses

Finally, self-centeredness causes unintentional offenses. Have you ever offended your spouse, or someone else, when you didn't remotely intend to? Maybe you even thought you were doing the right thing? I certainly have. In fact, there are even examples in the Bible of such unintentional offenses. In Galatians 2:11-14, there is a story of just such an offense. These scriptures tell the story of how Peter offended Paul and a group of Gentile believers. Peter offended them due to a difficult situation he found himself in. Traditionally, Jews did not associate with Gentiles. However, Peter, in order to minister to the Gentiles, put aside his traditions and began spending time with the Gentiles and even eating his meals with them. No doubt the Gentiles enjoyed the friendship of this great man of God. Then some Jewish believers from Jerusalem came to visit. Peter was concerned that he would offend their sense of Jewish tradition, and that they would think less of him because of his close associations with the Gentiles; after all, the Jewish Old Covenant law said that Jews were not supposed to associate with Gentiles.

So, what did he do? He stopped socializing and eating with the Gentiles. He simply did what he thought was best to keep from offending the Jews. However, he did not consider how the Gentiles would feel about his sudden change in behavior. Paul rebuked Peter in front of everyone for doing this.

Peter unintentionally offended Paul and the Gentiles when he did what he thought was best to keep the high regard of the Jews. I can well imagine that Peter was surprised at the reaction that Paul and the Gentile believers had toward his actions.

There are many other Biblical examples of such offenses. Think of David and King Saul; King Saul was offended with David and tried to kill him even when David had done nothing wrong. (See 1 Samuel 19:1) Remember the patriarch Joseph and his brothers? The brothers got offended with Joseph and sold him into slavery. (See Genesis 37:28) Joseph's only offense was having a dream that his brothers did not like.

These are the effects of self-centeredness. First, it is the destroyer of marriage relationships. Second, it destroys success in your life. Third, self-centeredness leads to manipulation of your spouse. Fourth, it causes all the irritations in marriage that are really just symptoms of self-centeredness. Fifth, it steals your joy or happiness. Finally, it causes offenses, intentional and unintentional. Trying to treat the symptoms will not save your marriage, but it will frustrate you. Given all of this, who in their right mind would want to be self-centered?

The Magnitude of The Problem

OK, we've established that self-centeredness is the root problem. Now, I want you to understand just how big a deal it is; I want you to see how important this issue is to God and to your marriage. In Matthew, Jesus tells us what the greatest commandment is.

Matthew 22:36-40 (NKJV)

"Teacher, which is the great commandment in the law? Jesus said to him, 'You shall love the Lord your God with all your heart, with all your soul, and with all your mind.' This is the first and great commandment. And the second is like it: 'You shall love your neighbor as yourself.' On these two commandments hang all the Law and the Prophets."

Essentially what Jesus is telling you to do is to love God first, above all else, and to love others second. If God is first and everybody else is second, that leaves you in last place. Earlier we defined other-centeredness as giving no thought to yourself and putting others above you on the priority list. Do you see what I see? The greatest commandments are really commands to be other centered—to put God and others higher on your priority list than you put yourself! Jesus says that all the law and prophets hang on these two commandments. Think about that! Could it really be that the aim of all the law and all the prophets—the entire Old Testament—was simply to defeat self-centeredness? I believe the answer is yes.

This shows the importance of overcoming self-centeredness; this shows how big an issue it really is. The two greatest commandments deal directly and solely with it. It is also mentioned in Philippians.

> Philippians 2:3-4 (NAS)
> *Do nothing from selfishness or empty conceit, but with humility of mind regard one another as more important than yourselves; do not merely look out for your own personal interests, but also for the interests of others."*

Here again is another scripture telling you to be other-centered. Think about all of the scriptures that tell you to crucify the flesh, die to self, put off the old man and so on. All of these are dealing with the issue of self-centeredness. If God addresses it so many times and calls it one of the two greatest commandments, it must be very important.

Genesis 3: 5 – 6, is another Biblical example of just how important this issue of self-centeredness is. These scriptures tell the story of Eve's conversation with the serpent. Satan in the guise of the serpent is trying to entice Eve to eat from the tree of the knowledge of good and evil, the one and only tree God had commanded Adam and Eve not to eat from. The scripture says that Eve saw that the fruit was appealing to her eye (it looked good), would be good to eat, and it would make her like God (according to Satan). So, she ate some and gave some to Adam who ate some also. (It is interesting that we tend to blame Eve for mankind's fall, but the Bible says Adam was there with her! Look it up in Genesis 3:6.) As a result of Adam and Eve's actions, they offended God, got put out of the Garden of Eden, and death entered the human race. Yes, God had said not to eat the fruit of this one tree, but when Eve saw that its fruit was pretty and looked good to eat, she disregarded God's instructions and ate some anyway. Satan appealed to her "self" to convince her to eat the fruit.

It is for your benefit and protection that God has commanded you to be other-centered. James tells us just how serious the consequences of self-centeredness are.

> James 4:17 (NAS)
> *"Therefore, to one who knows the right thing to do, and does not do it, to him it is sin."*

Not only is self-centeredness a very important issue with God and the destroyer of relationships, but it is also a violation of the two greatest commandments and, as such, it is a sin. It is the greatest obstacle to having a good marriage relationship. In fact, it is even the reason that Adam and Eve ate the fruit which resulted in man's fall. This is the enormous magnitude of self-centeredness.

The Danger of The Problem

There is a danger with self-centeredness. The danger is simply that you tend not to see your own self-centeredness as a problem. Despite what you just read above, you may be thinking, "I don't have a problem with self-centeredness." But look at what Isaiah has to say about this.

> Isaiah 53:6 (NIV)
> *"We all like sheep have gone astray, each has turned to his own way."*

Each of us has turned to our own way, which is to say that we are all doing what we want or being self-centered. Thus, everyone (including you and I) is self-centered at least to some degree, and everyone has the problem.

Proverbs 21:2 (NAS)

"Every man's way is right in his own eyes, but the Lord weighs the hearts."

This describes exactly how we tend to feel about our own self-centeredness. We understand why we act the way that we do, and therefore our actions, even our self-centered actions, seem justified. Our ways seem right in our own eyes. Since our actions are justified in our own mind, we do not see them as a problem, much less a sin. But God weighs our heart. He looks at our motives for why we do the things we do.

Do you remember the examples of offenses we talked about earlier? Eve thought eating the fruit seemed justified. After all, Satan said it looked good to eat and would make her like God. Peter did not want to offend the Jews or for them to think less of him. This is a perfectly logical reason to withdraw from eating with the Gentiles. In each of these cases the self-centered action that caused offense seemed to justify committing the self-centered act. None of them saw their action as a problem. But, of course hindsight is 20 - 20, and we now know that they were acting with a self-centered motive. No matter how justified it seemed, the action was still a sin and it was still wrong.

Here is another example to illustrate this point. Once upon a time, I came home from work. I was tired; I'd had a full day; I'd had my fill of people.... I just wanted to get a few minutes alone, read the paper, and relax. But Rebekah said to me almost as soon as I walked in the door, "Honey, let's talk." "About what?" I asked. "Just about things," she replied. "Well, OK," I said with obvious lack of enthusiasm. She talked for a while and I mostly listened offering a grunt once in a while. Finally, I asked, "Are you about done?" Of course, that was a stupid thing to say. Rebekah got mad and huffed out of the room. I was thinking, "What's wrong with her?"

Can you see my self-centered attitude in this example? When I came home, I was only thinking of myself, and what would please me. I gave no thought to Rebekah and what she might want or need from me. It was my self-centeredness that caused this conflict.

Let's look at another example. Suppose you are an individual who has suffered from some tragic circumstance like abuse, neglect, or divorce. Oftentimes people who go through such difficulties put up emotional walls to keep anyone from getting close enough to hurt them again. They learn to look out for number one. They begin taking advice from the world and start thinking that they must find happiness for themselves because no one else is going to make them happy.

Putting up these walls and looking out for number one is a defense mechanism they are using to avoid getting hurt again. But these walls make it very difficult for them to make and trust friends. It also makes it difficult for them to be truly intimate with their spouse. Such actions from a hurting person are very understandable. However, as justifiable as it may seem, this person is acting self-centeredly.

Seeking to please or to protect yourself at the expense of your marriage, even when it is due to past hurts, is self-centered. Such a person is putting their needs and desires above everyone else's. No matter how justified it seems, it is wrong. Although these people have real hurts to deal with and healing must take place, it cannot be used to justify self-centeredness on their part. In short, self-centeredness can be dressed up in many ways, but it is still a sin and it is wrong.

That's the danger of self-centeredness; our actions usually seem so justified to us that we don't even see that we are acting with self-centered motives.

Does the fact that our actions seem justified excuse them? The answer is, of course, no. The Bible tells us, in Romans 1:20 that, "...men are without excuse." As much as we might like to try, we cannot justify our self-centered actions. Self-centeredness is a violation of God's greatest commandment, and there is no way to justify or excuse it. It can be dressed up to look pretty, but there is still no excuse.

The Deceptiveness of The Problem

In addition to seeming justifiable, self-centeredness is also very deceptive. It is deceptive in that it can give you short term, false pleasure. Proverbs speaks about this.

Proverbs 16:25 (NKJV)
"There is a way that seems right to a man, but its end is the way of death."

This scripture is talking about our self-centered way - the way that seems right to us. Our self-centered ways seem right because it often does provide short-term pleasure.

Many people agree with the old cliché, "If it feels good do it" or "how could something be wrong when it feels so right". We believe that if it feels good it must be the right thing to do. In the end, however, a person's single-minded seeking of pleasure leads to death. It kills the marriage relationship because it is contrary to God's nature which tells you to put your spouse above ourselves.

Hebrews 11:25 says that Moses chose rather "to suffer affliction with the people of God than to enjoy the passing pleasures of sin." Earlier, we looked at 1 Timothy 5:6, which plainly says that someone who serves themselves is dead even while they live. There is no true joy to be found in self-centered living.

My life used to be an excellent example of this fact. The chief thing I self-centeredly sought pleasure from was my career. I was constantly striving for a promotion, a raise, a new job making more money, a management position, a new professional certification, to complete some training course, to publish another professional article, or to publish a book. In all of these things I succeeded, but guess what? I would be happy for a few days, at most, and then the feeling of joy would dwindle away. Not wanting to lose that joy, I would begin the cycle again - trying to accomplish some new career goal to restore my happiness, thinking all the while that if the achievement were big enough, I would get lasting happiness. All of these actions were very self-centered. I was thinking of me (although I justified many of my actions by reasoning that my family would benefit from my success because I would eventually make more money). Because my actions focused on myself, I never found lasting happiness.

Many people have this problem. They are hooked on trying to please themselves by self-centered means. It is a lot like a drug addiction. When the first fix wears off, not wanting to lose the "high", they begin looking for the next fix. The "fix" for many people can be as different as people are themselves. It might be a new job or position, nice cars, more money, the right clothes, a new swimming pool, a nicer house, an exotic vacation, alcohol, the "right" friends, drugs, or maybe new sexual conquests. We think, "If only I had this, I'd be happy; If only I had that I'd be happy; If only I had this and that I'd be happy." I'm sure many of you can relate to this feeling. There is nothing wrong with having a nicer house or car, God just wants you to have the right heart motive for wanting these things.

Experience will prove, however, that none of these things can make you happy. Only a short-lived, false happiness can be achieved by self-centered means. True happiness can only be realized through the other-centeredness that results from a growing relationship with God.

The passing pleasures offered by the sin of self-centeredness are a trap!

The Burden

Improving the marriage relationship seems like very hard work. In fact, we generally think that all relationships require hard work to maintain. For example, our relationship with God requires that we spend time with Him in prayer and read the Bible to get to know Him better. It requires that we obey His commandments even when we really want to do something else. Similarly, your relationship with your spouse requires work. You have to spend time with your spouse getting to know them. You need to think of their needs and not only your own, and so on. All of this seems like a lot of work. We even say things like, "My marriage needs a lot of work" and we talk in terms of "maintaining my marriage." But 1 John says this is not how it should be.

1 John 5:3 (NIV)
"This is love for God: to obey His commands. And His commands are not burdensome."

I think all of us would agree that if we keep God's commandments, which would include putting our spouse above ourselves, we would have much better relationships. Again, this seems like hard work. But, the scripture says "God's commands are not burdensome." If keeping God's commands is not the burden, then what makes building and maintaining relationships seem like such hard work?

I want to show you an amazing Bible passage that answers this question. It is found in Joshua.

Joshua 15:13 & 14 (NAS)
"Now he gave to Caleb the son of Jephunneh a portion among the sons of Judah, according to the command of the Lord to Joshua, namely Kiriath-arba, Arba being the father of Anak (that is Hebron).

*And Caleb drove out from there the three sons of Anak: Sheshai and
Ahiman and Talmai, the children of Anak."*

You are probably wondering what in the world this has to do
with marriage relationships, but just keep reading. Caleb was one of
the original 12 scouts that Moses sent to spy out the Promised Land
when the children of Israel first arrived at the Jordan River. Of the
12 spies, only two, Caleb and Joshua, reported that they would be
able to conquer the land as God had said. The remaining ten did not
believe God and said they could not take the land because there
were fortified cities and giants (like the children of Anak) living
there. Because they did not believe God's promise, God sent the
Israelites to wander in the wilderness for 40 years. But, because
Caleb believed God, he was promised the land called Hebron, which
interestingly enough means "to socialize or have friendship,
communion with God, or an intimate relationship". After the forty
years of wandering were over, Caleb took Hebron. As we read
above, to take the land he had to defeat the giants Ahiman, Talmai,
and Sheshai, who were the children of Anak. It is interesting to note
what the names of each of these giants mean. Their literal and inferred
meanings are listed in the table below.1

Name	Literal Meaning	Inferred Meaning
Anak	Long neck	Self will
Ahiman	My brother's gift	Selfishness
Talmai	Digging a rut/ tradition	Self sufficiency
Sheshai	White linen	Self-righteousness

As you can see, Caleb had to defeat the giants of "self" to
receive God's best for him. Remember, the name Hebron means to
have a good and intimate relationship, particularly with God.

For Caleb to receive an intimate relationship with God he had to overcome self. I do not believe it is an accident in any way that these giant's names mean what they do. Just as self came between Caleb and God's best for him, so it is self that comes between you and God's best for you. It is self that makes God's commands seem burdensome. And most importantly, self is the root problem that can keep you from enjoying the marriage relationship that God wants you to have.

The Solution to the Problem

The solution to the problem is found in Matthew.

Matthew 10:39 (NIV)
"Whoever finds his life will lose it, and whoever loses his life for My sake will find it."

When this scripture speaks of one who "finds his life," it is talking about a person who is self-centeredly seeking to live their life their way – not God's way. In doing so they find their life for themselves, and the scripture says this person will lose their life - that is they will never achieve happiness or satisfaction. The person who loses his life for Jesus' sake is the person who gives up his self-centered wants and desires and puts God first and others second. The scripture says this person will find his life. This means he will find the lasting joy and pleasure in living that he has always been seeking. The way to achieve lasting happiness is to put God first and others second. This does not mean you have to give up your wants, needs, and desires. The Lord promises to take care of you. See the below scripture.

Psalm 23 (NKJV)
"The Lord is my shepherd, I shall not want."

Let me explain further. Joshua and Caleb wanted to go in and take the Promised Land. The other 10 spies said they could not take it. The children of Israel wound up wandering in the wilderness for 40 years. Joshua and Caleb had to go wander with them even though they wanted to take the land. God wanted them to take the land, but in order to get what God wanted them to have; those two guys had to stay with God's people until God said to go get it. Forty years later they were given the go ahead to take what God promised them. Don't you think that Joshua and Caleb wanted to figure out a way to get their inheritance that did not include waiting with the "unbelievers" for 40 years? Don't you think they might have had reason to blame the others for holding them back? Do you think they might have had to forgive them a lot before those 40 years were over? Absolutely! Their desire was the Promised Land. God's desire for them was the Promised Land. But they had to do it God's way.

What about us? God has redeemed us from the curse according to Galatians 3:13. One of our promises is that in place of poverty He has given us prosperity. So desiring prosperity is scriptural, but if I sacrifice my family and work 60 or 80 hours a week to get it that is not God's way. I can let my desire ruin my family, or I can trust God to meet my family's need, put my wife's desires above my own, and God will surely bring my desires (and needs and wants) to pass His way.

It takes faith - a decision to believe it is true just because God says it is. It is difficult at first to step out in faith, but as you exercise your faith it becomes stronger just like your muscles become stronger with exercise. Consistent exercise gives you the strength to do more and more with your muscles. This is also true with faith. It grows with exercise and you become able to do more and more with it.

Romans 8:5&6 (NIV)

"For those who live according to the sinful nature have their minds
set on what that nature desires; but those who live in accordance with
the Spirit have their minds set on what the Spirit desires. The mind
of sinful man is death, but the mind controlled by the Spirit is Life
and Peace."

The sinful nature in mankind desires to put self first; Paul spoke of it in Romans 7:23 (NAS) as "the law of sin which is in my members." God wants you to repent of self-centeredness and begin obeying the greatest commandments which instruct us to be other centered. In order to be transformed into an other-centered person, you must set your mind on Him and put Him first and others above yourself. Even though you are to put others above yourself, keep in mind that you are one flesh with your spouse (Genesis 2:24). This is the closest relationship any person can have with another person. Therefore, our spouse needs to be our second priority after God. Everyone else is a lesser priority than your spouse; this includes your children. By setting our minds on God and His commands and putting God and your spouse in their proper standing you will receive life and peace in your marriage as promised in Romans.

"What about me? If I put others first, who will take care of me?" This is a common concern that many people have, and you probably know the answer. In Philippians 4:12 (AMP), Paul says he has learned "the secret of facing every situation." In verse 13 he goes on to say, "I have strength for all things in Christ Who empowers me." In Romans 9:33, Paul wrote "he who believes in Him shall not be put to shame nor be disappointed." If you trust God, and do things His way, He will take care of you. You will be able to handle whatever comes and you won't be put to shame or disappointed. God will meet your needs and desires. That is good news!

These principles have proven true in my own life. I used to live my life for my own pleasure. If anyone else, like my wife, enjoyed themselves that was good, but it was not because of my efforts that they had a good time. This lifestyle led me to alcoholism, a failed marriage, and unhappiness. As the scripture says, I lost my life by trying to find it. Following my sinful nature was leading to disaster. But then, after God came into my life, I began to be less self-centered. I started trying to put others, including Rebekah, first. I began to try to find ways to please and to serve others. And above all, I tried to put God first. Rebekah did the same. She also sought to put God first and others above herself. As a result of our "losing our lives", God restored our marriage. This has been very fulfilling for us and we have found great joy in it. Truly, by losing our lives we have now found them, just as the scripture promises. God will do the same for you, if you lose your life for Him

Putting it to Work in Day to Day Life

Throughout this book we will provide exercises to help you apply these principals. After all, James 1:22 (NKJV) exhorts us to be "doers of the Word, and not hearers only, deceiving yourselves". We hope that you and your spouse will both participate in these exercises. However, you can do them alone. Follow the guidelines listed and read the entire exercise before beginning so you understand completely before starting.

I want to look at three scriptures that illustrate how to avoid being self-centered. Many people learned this first scripture in nursery school; it is what we call the "Golden Rule." It is found in Matthew.

Matthew 7:12 (NKJV)

"Therefore, whatever you want men to do to you, do also to them, for this is the Law and the Prophets."

If you can treat other people the way you want to be treated, that will go a long, long way toward helping you avoid self-centeredness.

Next, let's look at Galatians.

Galatians 5:13 – 14 (AMP)

For you, brethren, were [indeed] called to freedom; only [do not let your] freedom be an incentive to your flesh and an opportunity or excuse [for selfishness], but through love you should serve one another. For the whole Law [concerning human relationships] is complied with in the one precept, You shall love your neighbor as [you do] yourself."

This is one of my favorite scriptures because it says so much in one verse. Don't be selfish. Instead love and serve others. This summarizes the whole law regarding how to have good human relationships. Do you want good relationships? Just do this – walk in love – prefer your spouse over yourself.

Finally, let's look at Philippians.

Philippians 2:2 (NKJV)

"Fulfill my joy by being like-minded, having the same love, being of one accord, of one mind."

What is he saying in verse 2? He is saying to get along with each other - to have good relationships. Next, in verses 3 and 4, he tells us how to do it.

Philippians 2:3-4 (NKJV)

"Let nothing be done through selfish ambition or conceit, but in lowliness of mind let each esteem others better than himself. Let each

of you look out not only for his own interests, but also for the interests of others."

Allow me to paraphrase. To have good relationships, don't be selfish, but take care of others. That is what it all comes down to. In every situation, put the Golden Rule to work by putting yourself in the other person's shoes, and asking yourself, "If I were them, what would I want someone to do for me in this situation?" That is what you should do. For example, Rebekah might ask herself, "If I were Rick, what would I want done for me?" Ask the question and then do the answer.

Now, let me give you an example that applies these principles to avoid self-centeredness. Suppose you are driving your wife's car and it is low on gas. Should you fill it up before taking it home, or just leave it for her to fill up the next time she drives it? Put yourself in her shoes. What would you want her to do for you? You would probably like it if she would fill your car up instead of using all the gas and leaving it for you to deal with. You are free to leave it on empty; you won't go to hell if you do. But don't let that freedom be an excuse to do whatever you want. Go ahead and fill it up with gas. Esteem her opinion over yours; look out for her interests and not your own. Gas her car up!

Pay attention to this please -- the self-centeredness you must deal with is your own. You cannot correct your spouse's self-centeredness - you cannot change anyone. Your spouse's self-centeredness is between him or her and God. Possibly the worst thing you could do is begin pointing out to your spouse how they are self-centered. Keep the focus on you. Rebekah started doing this before I was born again; rather than pointing out what I was doing wrong, she kept the focus on her, and it changed me as much as it changed her. The fact that self-centeredness is the problem is a tool you have been given. You can use the tool like you would use a shovel, to help build. Or you could use that shovel to kill someone. Use it wisely.

A Thought

There is a specific situation I want to address in discussing self-centeredness.

If someone leaves their spouse and their kids, they might as well dispense with excuses and just tell them the truth. The truth is simply that they love themselves more than they love their spouse and kids. I'm not talking about abusive situations or situations where a spouse is involved in some sort of destructive behavior or marital infidelity. I'm talking about the situations you hear about where one day, out of the blue, someone says, "I don't love you anymore and I want a divorce." Maybe they want a divorce because they are tired of being married or want to play the field or whatever. In those situations, you might as well just look your spouse and kids in the eye and say, "I'm leaving because I love me more than I love you." If you are going to throw that kind of wrench into their lives, have the guts to be honest!

Conclusion

The first step in healing your marriage relationship is to recognize that self-centeredness is the problem. It is the destroyer of relationships and it causes all of the irritating symptoms in your marriage. It is dangerous in that we don't recognize our own self-centeredness. It is deceptive in that it can give false pleasure. It is what stands between us and the great marriage God has for us.

Many people are looking for some really deep, super spiritual revelation that will zap them and fix their marriage. I believe there isn't one. In fact, I believe there is no deeper spiritual truth than the revelation that self-centeredness is the problem.

Endnote:

[1] Regarding the inferred meanings of the names of the giants, Anak, Ahiman, Talmai, and Sheshai, I have two sources. The first is a sermon by the Reverend Ronald K. Gray. Second is the booklet titled "Victory Over Self" by Albert Benjamin Simpson, founder of the Christian and Missionary Alliance, Nyack College, and Alliance Theological Seminary..

Chapter 2

FORGIVENESS -
A KEY TO UNITY

I T happened one Sunday morning not too long after Rebekah and I had gotten saved. We got into an argument before church. We were both offended, and we were not over it by the time we got to church. Normally, I helped usher and receive the offering, and occasionally the Pastor would even ask me to pray over the offering. Because of what had happened between Rebekah and me—because of the offense between us—I felt horrible. I knew that I could not serve in the church this morning as I usually did; I felt it would be wrong for me to do so. I asked the head usher to get someone else to help that day. This awful feeling did not leave me until I had talked to Rebekah after church and forgiveness took place.

In his book, *Mere Christianity*, C.S. Lewis said that forgiveness, particularly where one's enemies are concerned, is the most unpopular Christian Doctrine. I agree. Probably no other principal of Christianity is so simple to understand but so difficult to put into practice. However, just as forgiving others is an extremely important part of Christianity, forgiving your spouse is an extremely important prerequisite to a successful marriage relationship. In fact, it is the first thing that God dealt with

Rebekah and me about when He began leading us through the restoration of our marriage.

We had a lot of forgiving to do, too. The last chapter of this book is our testimony. If you read it, you'll see that we created a lot of hurts for each other. Every time we would try to work on our relationship, all of those past hurts would roll up like a tidal wave. Forgiveness was an important step in dealing with that mountain of past hurt once and for all. It was a hard thing to do too; neither one of us wanted to let go of those past hurts. We wanted to make the other person pay for what they had done to us.

That is exactly why forgiving others is so hard to swallow, because it goes totally against your human nature—or "the flesh." When someone hurts or offends you, your human nature screams out, "Revenge—get revenge! Hold it against them until they beg you to forgive them! Get mad. Get even! Make them pay!" I believe that everyone has, at one time or another, had similar thoughts to those I just described. This is your fleshly nature rising up in anger at the person who offended you. Oddly enough, this reaction often seems to be most intense when it is your spouse who does the offending. This is at least due in part because your spouse is usually the person that you expect to know you best, understand you best, and accept you and love you just as you are. Most of us went into marriage assuming that our spouse would treat us right. We assumed that they – above all people – would meet our needs and take care of us (note that this is a very self-centered attitude!). Because of this high expectation, you set a higher standard for them -- you expect them to never make a mistake. When they do, you are hurt more deeply and react more strongly and more angrily than when others offend you who are not so close to you.

Even outside of marriage relationships, unforgiveness can be ugly. I know a man, now in his forties, who at 14 years of age offended one of his relatives by pulling a childish prank. The relative never forgave this young man. Now, nearly 30 years later, they can be in the same room at a family function and never look at, or speak to, each other. That is unforgiveness at work!

We have all probably known people in similar circumstances. Person A gets offended at person B and carries a grudge against person B to the grave. Sometimes they don't even remember what the offense was about, but they sure remember that they are carrying a grudge and they aren't about to let go of it. It isn't even that unusual to meet grown children who have not spoken to their parents in years because of unforgiveness. Likewise, it isn't unusual to meet husbands and wives, still married, who will go days without speaking to each other because they have gotten into the habit of harboring offenses against one another.

If it weren't for forgiveness, your relationship with God could never have been restored. The same is true in marriage; forgiveness, no matter how unpopular or difficult, is essential to a successful marriage. Your marriage cannot be restored as long as unforgiven offenses remain.

This was true for Rebekah and me. We had offended each other so much and so often that we could not carry on anything even close to a normal conversation; talking about the smallest subject would lead to a big fight. Literally, every time one of us opened our mouths to communicate, it was as if the other took that as an opportunity to attack and start an argument. The offenses and unforgiveness had totally closed us to one another. We were very bitter toward each other and very unhappy. Unforgiveness was definitely hindering our relationship.

It is obvious from all of this that unforgiveness is a big, big problem in relationships. It absolutely must be dealt with in order to have the marriage relationship God wants you to have.

As you read the rest of this chapter, keep this in mind: forgiveness helps keep you in a right relationship with God and others. Unforgiveness separates you from God and others. More specifically, forgiveness keeps you in a right relationship with your spouse. Unforgiveness separates you from your spouse.

In this chapter, we will discuss the importance of forgiveness, the consequences of unforgiveness, how often you should forgive, what you should forgive, and who you should forgive.

The Importance of Forgiveness

The importance of forgiveness in your relationship with God and with other people simply cannot be overemphasized. The Bible plainly teaches that forgiveness is critical to restoring our relationship with God. Let's look at Colossians.

> Colossians 1:13 & 14 (AMP)
> *"[The Father] has delivered and drawn us to Himself out of the control and the dominion of darkness and has transferred us into the kingdom of the Son of His love. In whom we have our redemption through His Blood, [which means] the forgiveness of our sins."*

This scripture says you are saved by the forgiveness of your sins. The word "redemption" as used in this scripture means to be placed back into right relationship with God. (See also Luke 1:77, Acts 2:38, and Eph. 1:7.) By going to the cross and shedding His blood, Jesus made provision for the forgiveness of your sins. If not for this, you could not be a Christian and have a restored relationship with God. Therefore, the importance of forgiveness in your relationship with God is obvious.

The Bible also teaches that forgiveness restores relationships between people. Look at Ephesians.

> Ephesians 4:31 & 32 (NKJV)
> *"Let all bitterness, and wrath, and anger, and clamor, and evil speaking, be put away from you with all malice: and be ye kind one to*

another, tenderhearted, forgiving one another, even as God for Christ's sake hath forgiven you."

These scriptures tell you that you can get rid of bitterness, rage, and anger by being kind, compassionate and <u>forgiving</u> one another. Now look at Matthew.

Matthew 5:23 & 24 (KJV)
"Therefore if thou bring thy gift to the altar, and there rememberest that thy brother hath ought against thee; Leave there thy gift before the altar, and go thy way; first be reconciled to thy brother, and then come and offer thy gift."

Based on this scripture you can see that not only is forgiveness essential to restoring your relationship with God, but it is also just as important to restoring relationships between people, including your marriage relationship.

Unforgiveness is like an impassable roadblock or an impenetrable wall in your relationship. You cannot get to intimacy while this roadblock remains. Forgiveness helps remove the wall; it is like a big spiritual hammer that knocks down the wall created by unforgiveness.

I'm sure you have certainly heard the expression "sweep it under the rug". That is what most people want to do when they are offended by their spouse. They would rather just sweep it under the rug than confront their spouse about the offense. Sometimes, they will be mad for a while, but they usually get over being mad. Then, the anger is forgotten for the time being and they do not want to deal with the problem because it is easier to ignore it. It is easier to "sweep it under the rug". When you sweep dirt under the rug, you can no longer see it, but it is still there. Sooner or later you will have to deal with it because it will eventually pile up and create a bump in your rug. As time goes by and you sweep more and more under the rug you gradually get bigger and bigger bumps. At last, when the bumps are big enough, you are bound to trip over them. The only safe thing to do is get rid of the dirt.

The same is true in marriage. You can ignore the offense and pretend it did not happen, but it still makes a "bump" in your relationship. Sooner or later you will trip over that bump. Old offenses will come crashing back in—anger will be stoked back up into a nice hot fire. The only safe thing to do is get rid of the offense. A tool you can use to do this is forgiveness.

Consequences of Unforgiveness

As you saw in Ephesians 4:31 & 32 above, God expects you to forgive others—that includes your spouse. In fact, the consequences of not forgiving others are very severe. In the preceding section we took a look at one consequence of unforgiveness toward others; it hinders your relationship with that person. This is a considerable consequence if your goal is to have a good marriage. It means you have to forgive your spouse to have that good relationship.

However, that is not the only consequence of unforgiveness. There are other major consequences attached to not forgiving other people. One is found in Matthew.

Matthew 6: 14 & 15 (KJV)

"For if ye forgive men their trespasses, your heavenly Father will also forgive you. But if ye forgive not men their trespasses, neither will your Father forgive your trespasses."

Oh my! This scripture says that if you do not forgive people who offend you, God will not forgive you for your sins. (See also Mark 11:25 & 26.) So, not only does unforgiveness hinder your relationship with others, but it also hinders your relationship with God as well. He will not forgive you unless you forgive others; God said this. It is in the Bible. You just saw it. We are not making it up. If you won't forgive your spouse, God can't forgive you! Based on this it is obvious that God is very serious about this forgiveness thing; he really expects His children to practice it.

I have experienced this personally, and maybe you have too. I told the story at the start of this chapter about the time Rebekah and I went to church mad at each other. That affected me to the point that I was simply not able to serve in our church that day. Think about that! What divine appointment might I have missed due to that one offense? What opportunity to help someone, to sow a seed that would later bring something good, might I have missed? I'll never know. Maybe none, but on the other hand, I might have missed the opportunity of a lifetime. A lot of people won't even go to church if they get mad. Think about what you could miss by not going at all. It is much better to just forgive.

Another consequence of unforgiveness is it can cause bitterness. If you harbor it toward one person, you are more likely to get into unforgiveness with other people. The next thing you know, you are offended with everyone. Bitterness can result. Let's look at Hebrews.

Hebrews 12:14 & 15 (AMP)

"Strive to live in peace with everybody and pursue that consecration and holiness without which no one will [ever] see the Lord. Exercise foresight and be on the watch to look [after one another], to see that no one falls back from and fails to secure God's grace (His unmerited favor and spiritual blessing), in order that no root of resentment (rancor, bitterness, or hatred) shoots forth and causes trouble and bitter torment, and the many become contaminated and defiled by it--."

Note it tells us to live in peace and pursue holiness, so that we don't become bitter. Where there is unforgiveness there is no peace and there is no holiness, and eventually it will cause the bitterness referred to here. This unforgiveness and bitterness can grow until it can cause a person to basically get mad at, and hold a grudge against everyone, including their spouse and children.

Here again, you see that forgiveness is essential in both your relationship with God and in your relationship with your spouse. The truth is you cannot have a successful relationship with God or with your spouse until you put forgiveness to work in your life. Not only that, but it is also essential to your own inner peace. Without forgiveness you will ultimately become an angry person. If the unforgiveness persists, the anger will lead to bitterness.

That Sunday when Rebekah and I went to church mad, all three of these consequences of unforgiveness we mentioned earlier were in effect; it hindered my relationship with God, it hindered my relationship with Rebekah, and it stole my inner peace. At the time, I really did not understand what had happened, but now I do. My relationship with God had been hindered because of my unforgiveness toward Rebekah. My relationship toward Rebekah was hindered because we were not speaking and there was unforgiveness between us. As a result, I felt horrible inside (no peace) and was unable to do anything. It wasn't until we reconciled that things were made right.

Believe it or not, there are even more consequences linked to unforgiveness.

The parable of the sower reveals another consequence of unforgiven offenses.

Mark 4:5, 16, & 17 (AMP)
"(vs. 5) Other seed [of the same kind] fell on ground full of rocks, where it had not much soil; and at once it sprang up, because it had no depth of soil;

(vs. 16) And in the same way the ones sown upon stony ground are those who, when they hear the Word, at once receive and accept and welcome it with joy;

(vs. 17) And they have no real root in themselves, and so they endure for a little while; then when trouble or persecution arises on account of the Word, they immediately are offended (become displeased, indignant, resentful) and they stumble and fall away."

In verse five, Jesus is telling the parable of the sower to the public at large. In verses 16 and 17, he is explaining the meaning of the parable to the disciples. It says that people—even those who receive the Word—get offended when trouble comes, and then they stumble and fall away. God's Word is the best seed a sower can sow; however, offense can choke the seed of the Word and cause it to not produce anything.

The bottom line here for us is this: offenses keep you from receiving from God. If offense chokes the seed of the Word—it will also choke the seed that you sow and keep it from producing a harvest in your life. You can sow a seed of something good in your marriage, maybe doing something nice for your spouse. But, if you do and there are unforgiven offenses in your life, your harvest will probably be very small, if you have any harvest at all. Offense chokes your seed from producing a harvest of good fruit in your life.

Matthew tells about a time when Jesus was preaching and ministering in His hometown. Take a look at what happened.

Matthew 13:54 - 57 (NKJV)

"When He had come to His own country, He taught them in their synagogue, so that they were astonished and said, Where did this Man get this wisdom and these mighty works? Is this not the carpenter's son? Is not His mother called Mary? And His brothers James, Joses, Simon, and Judas? And His sisters, are they not all with us? Where then did this Man get all these things? So they were offended at Him. But Jesus said to them, A prophet is not without honor except in his own country and in his own house. Now He did not do many mighty works there because of their unbelief."

Evidently the hometown folks knew Jesus and thought something like this, "Who does this guy think he is coming here and ministering to us. Why I remember when he was just a kid." So, they got offended with Jesus. The result was that they could not believe in his ministry and therefore could not receive from him. No doubt there were some sick people there, maybe some lame, maybe even some demon possessed. Did they need what Jesus had to offer? Yes! Could they get it? No! Why? Because of their offense. Offense keeps you from receiving from God.

Guess what? There are still more consequences. Jesus tells some people the following interesting information about how they treat other people and what God thinks of it.

Look at the below scripture.

Matthew 25: 42 – 45 (NKJV)

"I was hungry and you gave Me no food; I was thirsty and you gave Me no drink; I was a stranger and you did not take Me in, naked and you did not clothe Me, sick and in prison and you did not visit Me. Then they also will answer Him, saying, "Lord, when did we see You hungry or thirsty or a stranger or naked or sick or in prison, and did not minister to You? Then He will answer them, saying, Assuredly, I say to you, inasmuch as you did not do it to one of the least of these, you did not do it to Me."

Whatever you do to someone else, as far as God is concerned you are doing it to Him. That means if you hold unforgiveness against someone, God looks at it just as if you are holding unforgiveness against Him. That is serious stuff. Remember in Acts chapter 9:1 – 8 when Jesus met Saul on the road to Damascus? Jesus said, "Saul, why are you persecuting me?" Saul had been persecuting Christians, not Jesus. But Jesus looked at it just as if Saul was persecuting Him. Do you want to hold a grudge against God? I don't!

Finally, unforgiveness allows Satan to get an advantage over you. This is made very plain in 2 Corinthians.

2 Corinthians 2:10-12 (AMP)
"If you forgive anyone anything, I too forgive that one; and what I have forgiven, if I have forgiven anything, has been for your sakes in the presence [and with the approval] of Christ (the Messiah), to keep Satan from getting the advantage over us; for we are not ignorant of his wiles and intentions. Now when I arrived at Troas [to preach] the good news (the Gospel) of Christ, a door of opportunity was opened for me in the Lord."

The Bible says that Satan's job is to kill, steal, and destroy (John 10:10); do you want to give him an advantage over you? I really doubt it. It is much, much better to just forgive.

That's it. We are done with consequences. I'm sure there are more, but this should be plenty to show you that unforgiveness is bad and forgiveness is good. To summarize, the consequences of unforgiveness are:

- It hinders your relationship with God
- It hinders your relationship with your spouse and with other people
- It prevents God from being able to forgive you
- It causes bitterness
- It chokes your seed
- It keeps you from receiving from God
- If you are offended with your spouse, you are offended with God as far as He is concerned.

I once heard it said like this. If I'm holding unforgiveness toward you, it is like me drinking poison and expecting you to die. That isn't going to happen. You are only hurting yourself, so stop drinking poison—start forgiving.

How Often Should You Forgive?

A common question people have is, "How often should I forgive my spouse for doing the same thing over and over again? It's like they never learn. When is enough, enough?"

This is a very appropriate question—one that many people have tried to figure out at one time or another. When Rebekah and I first began working to restore our marriage, we would often get into arguments and one of us would say, "You always do this or you always do that. How often do you expect me to forgive you for this?" I particularly remember that she felt (and the reality was that she was often right!) like I was putting other things - particularly work and career—over her and the kids. Whenever something came up at work, or I wanted to do something, or someone else needed something, I expected my family to just understand that I needed to take care of whatever situation had come up. To Rebekah, my actions said she was last on my priority list. Since it kept happening over and over, Rebekah believed it was a sign that there was little hope for our marriage. After all, how long could she reasonably be expected to put up with the same old stuff happening over and over?

What we did not know is that it takes time for people to change. Often your spouse will make the same mistakes over and over again even when it really is their desire to work things out. This is what was happening in our case. (Let me point out, however, that this should not be used as an excuse to cover up lack of effort. You should be making an effort to work on your relationship. You should not expect perfection from your spouse, but you can reasonably expect improvement.)

Other times your spouse may keep doing the same things over and over, claiming to want to change when in reality, they just want to get out of trouble for the moment. They actually intend to keep acting the same way they always have which will result in the offense being repeated. Asking for forgiveness in this way is just a short-term fix. In fact, it is really just a way to manipulate the situation. Expecting forgiveness without trying to change is self-centered. You are just looking out for yourself and trying to make things good for you. It's like a kid caught with his hand in the cookie jar; he is extremely sorry that he got caught and he wants Mommy to forgive him and not spank him, but he intends to do it again! He hasn't really changed. Many people in marriage are like this and it is, at best, a very short-term type of relief to your problems.

So again, this brings us back to the question, how often should you forgive your spouse when they offend you? Especially when they keep doing the same thing over and over. This same question was asked of Jesus in Matthew.

Matthew 18:21 & 22 (NKJV)
"Then Peter came to Him and said, "Lord, how often shall my brother sin against me, and I forgive him? Up to seven times?" Jesus said to him, "I do not say to you, up to seven times, but up to seventy times seven."

Look at this scripture in Luke.

Luke 17:4 (NKJV)
"And if he sins against you seven times in a day, and seven times in a day returns to you, saying, 'I repent,' you shall forgive him."

I believe Jesus was speaking figuratively here. He meant that we should forgive every time, no matter how often! Rebekah was tired of forgiving me for the same thing over and over, but she would forgive me again anyway. She forgave me because she knew the consequences of unforgiveness and because she had made a decision ahead of time to forgive. This act of forgiveness kept our relationship from exploding until we were able to deal with the underlying root problem, self-centeredness, which was the real cause of all the other problems in our relationship (refer back to Chapter 1, The Problem). Let me point out something else here, we both knew that without forgiveness, our relationship was over. You need to know that too! Without forgiveness your relationship has gone as far as it ever will. You must forgive —every time.

What Should You Be Willing To Forgive?

Here is another very relevant question that we are asked. "You don't know what they did to me. They did 'this or that horrible thing.' I just can't forgive them for that. Surely you don't think I should forgive them for that do you?"

Some offenses are much worse and much more damaging than others. Just where do you draw the line with this forgiveness thing? The answer to this question is found in Ephesians 4:32 and 1 John 1:9.

Ephesians 4:32 (NKJV)
"And be kind to one another, tenderhearted, forgiving one another, even as God in Christ forgave you."

Basically, this is saying that you should be willing to forgive others for the same things that God is willing to forgive you for. What is God willing to forgive you for? The answer is found in 1 John.

1 John 1:9 (NKJV)
"If we confess our sins, He is faithful and just to forgive us our sins and to cleanse us from all unrighteousness."

God forgives you for all of your unrighteousness. Taken together, these scriptures say that you are to forgive your spouse for EVERYTHING just as God forgives you for EVERYTHING. Did you get that? It doesn't matter how bad they have hurt you. God says you need to forgive them anyway.

Remember, earlier we discussed all the bad consequences of unforgiveness. By not forgiving everything you bring all of these consequences on yourself. Again, if you don't, it's like you drinking poison and expecting them to die. They won't die, you are only hurting yourself. You need to forgive.

Forgiving your spouse for everything is a critical step to bringing reconciliation, unity, and peace into your marriage relationship. You must forgive your spouse as often as necessary and for everything. You need to "walk in forgiveness." Basically, that means you live life prepared to forgive at all times.

Let me add here that you can forgive someone without remaining in an abusive or potentially harmful situation. Proverbs provides guidance for this type of situation.

Proverbs 14:7 (NKJV)
"Go from the presence of a foolish man, when you do not perceive in him the lips of knowledge."

If some "fool" is possibly endangering your safety or your life, I would advise you to forgive them but remove yourself from that situation.

Who Should You Forgive?

To have a reconciled marriage, you must obviously forgive your spouse for their offenses. In addition to your spouse, you often must also forgive others. Believe it or not, past offenses that were never dealt with through forgiveness can affect your marriage relationship today. Many of us were hurt by old boyfriends or girlfriends, parents, siblings, ex-spouses, or other people in our past. In a lot of cases these past offenses were never forgiven.

In my relationship with Rebekah, this was true. I had a relationship with an old girlfriend years ago. When we broke the relationship off, I was very hurt. I was so hurt that I did not date anyone else for nearly two years. I made a conscious decision that

I would never let anyone get close enough to hurt me like that again. When I met Rebekah, I carried that attitude with me. I would not let her get close to me. I kept her at a distance, and she knew it. I even told her that I loved her, but that I would never need her. I would not let myself t need her, because I did not want to set myself up for that kind of pain again. This is just an example of how past hurts can affect your relationship today.

I have talked to many people and found the same to be true. Hurts experienced in previous relationships and marriages affect how they relate to their spouse now. Most people react by being less willing to open up fully to their spouse. They don't want to be transparent because they fear being hurt again. People will only risk being transparent with someone they believe they can trust. Some people have been so hurt that they don't trust anyone. As a result, they aren't completely open with anyone. Past hurts may cause you to withhold trust from your spouse in some areas or, on the other hand, your spouse may be having the same problem. Hurt people tend to become suspicious of others and protective of themselves; as someone once said, hurting people hurt other people.

The bottom line is that hurting people tend to be self-centered people. They look out for number one and try to make sure that they do not get hurt again. This is understandable, but this self-protection is still self-centered. The process of healing those old hurts, and becoming an other-centered person, begins with forgiving those people who hurt you. Forgiving can be painful because at times it is like reliving those old hurts again—but in order to get free, in order to bring down those old walls, you need to forgive.

In addition to your spouse and other people, sometimes you must forgive yourself. Some people are ashamed of their past and that affects how they relate to their spouse now. Perhaps they were sexually promiscuous, and they are afraid their spouse will find out. Things may have happened to them that they had no control over such as molestation, rape, or abuse. Others may have severely offended their current spouse in some way and fear that their spouse will hold the offense against them forever. I knew one man who had an affair. He refused to try to save his marriage because he was afraid to face his sin. He thought that it was too great to overcome. He thought he and his wife could never get past it to get on with working toward having a better marriage. As professional hockey great Wayne Gretzky said, "You miss 100 percent of the shots you never take". I have known other married men who had an affair, received forgiveness from their wife, changed their life, and went on to have a good marriage. If you don't try, the failure is certain.

Romans 8:1 says, "...there is no condemnation for those who are in Christ Jesus". 2 Corinthians 5:17 says that "...old things have passed away and all things have become new". In 2 Corinthians 7:2 (KJV), the apostle Paul wrote, "...we have wronged no one, we have corrupted no man, we have defrauded no man." This is the same guy who persecuted the Christians—the same guy who had them thrown into prison and executed simply because they were Christians. How could he say that he had wronged no one? Because he understood the power of forgiveness and how it can affect our standing with God. I truly believe that many people need to get hold of this spiritual truth and forgive themselves. In God's eyes their record is clean, and that is the most important record.

What if They Don't Repent?

Here is another take on the issue of forgiveness for you to consider. We looked at Luke 17:4 above where it says that if the person who offended you repents you are to forgive them. What about those people who offend you and never ask for your forgiveness? I am sure you have experienced situations in which someone offended you and that person later apologized and asked for your forgiveness. On the other hand, I am also sure you have been offended by someone who did not ask for forgiveness. Maybe it happened with friends, back in high school, with co-workers, church family, even with your spouse today, or whatever. If you are like me, your personal experience proves it is a lot easier forgive someone who repents than it is to forgive people who do not.

It is not unusual for people to offend you in some way and never realize they have done anything. However, sometimes, people do not even care that they have offended you. Let's look at what the Bible says you are to do in this situation.

Mark 11:25 (KJV)
"And when ye stand praying, forgive, if ye have ought against any: that your Father also which is in heaven may forgive you your trespasses."

This scripture tells you to forgive. Did it say anyone had to repent? No! Clearly you are to forgive people whether or not they have asked you to. It says to forgive them—it does not say to forgive them if they repent. It is hard enough to forgive under the best of circumstances. It is harder still to forgive someone who has not asked you to forgive them and who may not even remotely care or feel sorry that they have hurt you. But for your own good, you cannot harbor unforgiveness against them. Remember, if you do not forgive them, God does not forgive you. Therefore, you need to forgive others even when they do not repent. You may be angry and hurt. You probably do not feel like forgiving them, but, you do not have to feel like forgiving. You simply need to make a decision to forgive them. So many people miss it right here because they think they have to feel it. How many times have you woke up in the middle of the night and you had to go to the bathroom but you just didn't feel like getting up? Do you just stay there and let "things" happen? No, you get up and take care of it whether you feel like it or not.

If you have ever wondered whether your spouse will offend you, Jesus provides the answer. In Luke, He said the following.

Luke 17:1-4 (NKJV)

"Then He said to the disciples, "It is impossible that no offenses should come, but woe to him through whom they do come! It would be better for him if a millstone were hung around his neck, and he were thrown into the sea, than that he should offend one of these little ones. Take heed to yourselves. If your brother sins against you, rebuke him; and if he repents, forgive him. And if he sins against you seven times in a day, and seven times in a day returns to you, saying, 'I repent,' you shall forgive him. "

So, yes, offenses are going to come—your spouse is going to offend you at some point. Your spouse is not perfect. If your spouse was perfect they would not need Jesus as a Savior. Make improvement your goal and expect it, but do not expect perfection. Realize that you will have opportunities to get offended. Remember, you will offend them to. Exercise the "Golden Rule" here.

As you read on in this scripture, He tells you how you are supposed to react to offenses. You should forgive –that is what you should do. That is the answer; you simply need to accept that people, including your spouse, will sooner or later offend you. You can make a "BIG" decision now that when this happens, you will forgive.

I have heard some people who think that to be offended is a sin. I do not believe this is correct; getting offended is a reaction that we have when we encounter circumstances we don't like. Jesus didn't say it was a sin. However, what you do with the offense could be a sin. For example, if you carry a grudge and refuse to forgive, that is sin.

Based on the scriptures we have looked at, the Bible teaches that you must forgive others. The Bible also teaches that you can do all things through Christ who strengthens you (Philippians 4:13). In most cases you will not feel like forgiving someone, but you need to do it anyway. Pray and say, "I forgive so and so in

Jesus name." After doing this you need to accept, by faith, that you have forgiven that person. Even if your feelings haven't changed, you have made a decision. If you will stick with your decision, and don't dwell on unforgiving thoughts or on the offense, your feelings will eventually change. When thoughts of unforgiveness come, remind yourself of the decision you made.

Rebekah and I have experienced this in our own lives. In the early years, we inflicted a lot of hurt and pain on each other as you can read in our testimony at the end of this book. When you have a mountain of unforgiveness and pain, you think there is no way you will ever be able to overcome it. But today, when Rebekah and I tell others about what we went through —the things we did to each other— and how we came out, it's as if it happened to someone else. We remember the events, but the hurt is completely gone. It's almost like something we saw in a movie that didn't really happen to us, but it did happen to us. We are completely healed. The healing started with a decision.

At the beginning of this chapter, I told you that the bottom line is that if it were not for forgiveness of our sins, our relationship with God would never have been restored. The same is true in marriage. Forgiveness, no matter how unpopular or difficult the doctrine, is essential. Forgiveness is not optional. You must practice it to have the marriage relationship God means you to have.

Putting Forgiveness to Work In Your Relationship - A Practical Application

Here is how you can put forgiveness to work in your relationship. Do this exercise ALONE – not with your spouse. First, get a pencil and paper. Now, pray and ask God to reveal to you offenses your spouse has committed against you that you have not forgiven them for. Think on this question and write down what the Lord brings to your mind. Do not labor over it. Just trust God to reveal the offenses to you and write those down. Next, ask God to reveal to you any offenses caused by other people such as old boyfriends/girlfriends, ex-spouses, parents, friends, siblings and so on. Here again, think on this and write down what the Lord brings to your mind. Finally, ask God if there is any area in your life in which you need to forgive yourself. Again, think on the question and write down what God shows you.

Next, you should pray and ask God to help you forgive each of the offenses and people you have listed. (Remember, forgiveness is a decision and not a feeling. God can give you the grace to forgive even in situations where you may not want to.) Then you need to pray and forgive all of those people and all of the offenses the Lord revealed to you. Remember, you may not feel like forgiving these people, but to get on with building your marriage you must. When you pray, forgive each person for the offense in Jesus' name.

For example, pray, "Father in Jesus name I forgive (insert name) for (insert the action requiring forgiveness)." Pray over each person and over each offense on your list in this way. As you finish praying over each one, mark it off your list. No doubt the devil will try to resurrect unforgiveness toward others in you, but remind the devil of what you have done. You made a decision to forgive. Also, if both you and your spouse are doing this exercise, agree not to look at each other's lists. If for some reason you happen to find your spouse's list, don't read it. It wouldn't serve any purpose and it would create a lot of strife.

Over the next several days and even weeks, memories of these offenses may crop up, and you will be tempted to take up unforgiveness against those people again. When this happens remind the devil you have already forgiven these people that were on your list, and that you are free from unforgiveness and the bondage it brings. There is no need to hang on to the past – you need to press toward the future. Do not dwell on these past offenses or let yourself think about them—simply say, "No. I have forgiven so-and-so for that offense and it is over and past in Jesus' name."

If you think on these past offenses enough you will get mad all over again which starts the cycle of unforgiveness all over again. You can make a decision to forgive and forget just like God forgives and forgets. If the offense comes to your mind, think about something else on purpose. Refuse to think about the offense longer than to remind yourself that is in the past and under the Blood of Jesus. The pain may still be there for a while, but it will go away if you stay in forgiveness (Ephesians 4: 31 & 32). One last thing, make sure you do not talk about these offenses with someone else. This brings it back to life in your mind and before you know it you will be mad all over again and back into unforgiveness. If there are certain people that usually remind you of these things, you need to change the conversation and hold your ground, do whatever it takes not to talk about it. You may need to politely tell them that that particular subject is off limits and to please not bring it up again. This will keep you in forgiveness. That is the end of this exercise.

So, make the big decision now, that when offenses occur, you will forgive. Then you won't have to try to talk yourself into forgiving when you're mad or offended, you'll just forgive, like that's the only option available. Because in reality, it is.

Jeremiah 4:14 (NLT)
"O Jerusalem, cleanse your hearts that you may be saved. How long will you harbor your evil thoughts?"

Notice that **you** are harboring these evil thoughts. The Amplified translation refers to them as "iniquitous and grossly offensive thoughts." If you are doing the "harboring", then you can do the "un-harboring." All that is required is a decision to forgive, let go of offenses, and stick to the decision.

The importance of forgiveness in a marriage relationship

cannot be over emphasized. Just as forgiveness is a key to restoring your relationship with God, so it is a key to restoring your marriage relationship. However, (and most people are surprised at this) forgiveness alone does not equal reconciliation or restoration of a marriage. Just because you have forgiven someone does not mean you have to open yourself up to that person and let them hurt you again. Forgiveness is more about getting rid of the damaging effects that unforgiveness can cause to you. For reconciliation and restoration to take place, something else is necessary. That is the subject of the next chapter.

Chapter 3

BREAKING UP
YOUR FALLOW GROUND

ONCE there were two farmers whose fields were right next to each other. One farmer was a hard working man. The other was lazy. He was always looking for the easiest way to do things. During the fall and winter, their fields had lain fallow and gotten weedy and hard. When spring came the hard working farmer got out his tractor and plowed up his field. By plowing, he broke up the ground and turned it over so that all of the weeds were eliminated. Then he hooked up a harrow to the tractor and used it to further break the ground up into very fine pieces. When he was finished, the soil was nice and soft; the perfect environment for young roots to grow into. Finally, he laid out rows in the garden, fertilized the soil, and planted his vegetables. The lazy farmer stood leaning over the fence and watched his sweating neighbor do all of this work.

"He takes this stuff too seriously," thought the lazy farmer. "Not me." With that, he got out his riding mower and mowed down the weeds on his garden. He then got a sharp stick and poked holes into the hard fallow soil. He dropped a few vegetable seeds into each hole and kicked dirt over the holes with his foot. His work was completed with far less effort than his neighbor had put forth. "That's good enough," he thought to himself. "Why go to all that extra effort." The lazy farmer enjoyed the rest of the afternoon idling away his time on the back porch and keeping an eye on his busy neighbor's progress. Occasionally, he would shake his head and chuckle to himself.

Now, let me ask you a question. Which of these two farmers do you suppose had the greatest harvest at the end of the summer? The answer is obvious—the hard working farmer. He took the time to break up the fallow ground before he tried to plant. He knew that he could expect to receive no harvest until the ground was properly prepared.

It is pretty obvious that the lazy farmer will have a terrible harvest and is likely to go hungry.

You cannot sow seeds and expect a good harvest if the soil is not prepared. Yet, many people do this very thing in their marriage relationship. They are trying to build a good relationship, maybe they are even trying to use the Word of God as the basis for their relationship, but as time goes by, problems still crop up in their relationship. When this happens they might think that the Word doesn't work. That is totally incorrect. The Word does work. It is the condition of the "soil" that is the problem.

Let us look at a couple of scriptures.

Hosea 10:12 & 13 (NKJV)

"Sow for yourselves righteousness; Reap in mercy; Break up your fallow ground, for it is time to seek the Lord, Till He comes and rains righteousness on you. You have plowed wickedness; you have reaped iniquity. You have eaten the fruit of lies, because you trusted in your own way, in the multitude of your mighty men."

Now look at this.

Jeremiah 4:3 (NKJV)

"For thus says the Lord to the men of Judah and Jerusalem: Break up your fallow ground, And do not sow among thorns."

Finally, let's look at another scripture from Jeremiah.

Jeremiah 12:13 (NKJV)
"They have sown wheat but reaped thorns; they have put themselves to pain but do not profit. But be ashamed of your harvest because of the fierce anger of the Lord."

The first two scriptures warn you to break up your fallow ground before sowing seed. Hosea and Jeremiah 12:13 go on tell you what kind of harvest you will get if you don't follow this instruction—a very bad harvest. What is fallow ground and why is God telling us to break it up? That is what we will look at in this chapter and we will see how it is essential to a restored marriage relationship.

What is Fallow Ground?

Fallow ground is ground that may once have been cultivated and planted but has been left untended and has now become grown up and choked with weeds and thorns. Even the best of gardens, if left untended for a year, will get hard and need to be broken up again to receive seed. Otherwise it will not produce a good harvest.

When God tells you to break up your fallow ground He is talking about your heart. The hard ground of your heart must be broken up to receive the seed. The seed God wants you to receive is His Word (the parable of the sower in Mark 4: 3 – 20 compares God's Word to seed). The fruit that He wants to be produced in your lives is Godly actions and attitudes.

I am a good example of someone who was hard hearted. Before becoming a Christian, I cared very little for anyone else. I cared about what was good for me and what would benefit me. The "what is in it for me?" mentality drove me to get an education, earn two professional certifications, seek promotions at work, etc.

It was about me, and what would benefit me, and what I wanted. I had a hard heart—I had fallow ground. None of the things I did was bad in and of itself, but my motive was wrong.

As I mentioned above, there are many similarities between fallow ground and a hardened heart. This is a very good example and we can learn a lot about ourselves by studying it.

Fallow ground is ground that has not been tilled in a long time. It is very hard. It needs to be broken up to a fine texture before it can receive seed. Imagine ground that is so hard and dry that it has cracks in it. You've probably seen pictures like that of African nations during a drought. That is fallow ground. It is hard and useless— nothing will grow in it. Now imagine potting soil; it is soft and lose. It is so soft that you can dig into it with your bare hands to plant the seeds. It is dark and rich with nutrients. With the right amount of water and sunlight, it will allow seeds to grow like crazy. Good seed in fallow ground will be wasted because it will not respond by growing. You can't even get the seed under the surface of the soil. Similarly, your heart gets hard and unresponsive; pride, selfishness, unforgiven offenses, all of these things can lead to a hard heart. A number of scriptures speak of hardness of hearts. Take a look at the following.

Mark 16:14 (NKJV)
"Later He appeared to the eleven as they sat at the table; and He rebuked their unbelief and hardness of heart, because they did not believe those who had seen Him after He had risen."

John 12:40 (NKJV)
"He has blinded their eyes and hardened their hearts, Lest they should see with their eyes, Lest they should understand with their hearts and turn, So that I should heal them."

A hardened heart stunts, or even stops, your spiritual growth. With a hard heart, you cannot receive the word of God and, therefore, the Word cannot grow and produce fruit in your life. Think of how important this is. Jesus said in John 15: 7 & 8 that if you abide in Him and His words abide in you, you can ask for anything and it will be done for you. It goes on to say that you will bear much fruit. Success in God pretty much depends on not having a hard heart.

Similarly, in a marriage relationship, a hard heart becomes insensitive to hear or to recognize the needs of your spouse. A hard heart is essentially a self-centered heart. It looks out for itself, not for others.

If a farmer wants a good crop he tills the ground, plants seeds, waters the ground, pulls the weeds, fertilizes as necessary, keeps the birds and animals away, and so on. It takes a fair amount of work to have a good crop. If a farmer wants to grow weeds—he does nothing. Just leave the field untended and it will grow a nice crop of weeds. Isn't it interesting that to have an abundant crop of something useful, it takes work, but to have an abundant crop of something useless or even harmful, neglect is required? The same is true in marriage.

If seeds sown on fallow ground are not killed by the hardness of the ground, they are likely to be killed by all of the weeds growing there or else eaten by birds. As you saw above, Jeremiah 4:3 tells us that we should not sow among thorns. In Jeremiah 12:13 we see the results of sowing among thorns and not breaking up the fallow ground. Here God says His people have sown wheat but reaped thorns; if you sow good seed among weeds, you are wasting the seed and will only reap weeds. Good fruit and vegetables die without cultivation. Weeds, on the other hand, thrive without cultivation. Weeds are a product of neglect. These weeds in the fallow ground of our hearts are what keep our marriage relationship from growing. The weeds I am talking about are self-centeredness and its fruit which is listed below.

Galatians 5:16 and 19 – 21 (MSG)

"My counsel is this: Live freely, animated and motivated by God's Spirit. Then you won't feed the compulsions of selfishness. It is obvious what kind of life develops out of trying to get your own way all the time: repetitive, loveless, cheap sex; a stinking accumulation of mental and emotional garbage; frenzied and joyless grabs for happiness; trinket Gods; magic-show religion; paranoid loneliness; cutthroat competition; all-consuming-yet-never-satisfied wants; a brutal temper; an impotence to love or be loved; divided homes and divided lives; small-minded and lopsided pursuits; the vicious habit of depersonalizing everyone into a rival; uncontrolled and uncontrollable addictions; ugly parodies of community. I could go on."

This bad fruit, coupled with past sins you may have committed, are the weeds that can choke out any good fruit that may try to grow in your life. Fallow ground is unfruitful. Good seed and showers are wasted on it. Like the lazy farmer, you cannot reasonably expect to have a fruitful marriage relationship if you have not broken up the fallow ground of your heart.

A key to a good marriage is to break up the fallow ground of your heart and get rid of the weeds. Only then can you receive seed (God's Word), begin living the fruitful life, and enjoying the marriage relationship God wants you to have.

A hard heart will lead to alienation from your spouse and ultimately to divorce. Jesus said so. Look at Matthew.

Matthew 19:8 (NKJV)

"He said to them, "Moses, because of the hardness of your hearts, permitted you to divorce your wives, but from the beginning it was not so."

No doubt about it. A hard, selfish heart is death to a marriage relationship.

What Does Breaking Up Your Fallow Ground Mean?

Very simply, breaking up your fallow ground means to bring your heart to a humble and contrite state. I believe that many people do not like the words humble and contrite simply because they really don't know what they mean from a Biblical perspective. We have placed a negative connotation on being humble and contrite that is not scriptural at all. To be humble simply means to be submitted to God. To be contrite means to realize that you have no excuses for your sins, and to admit that what God shows us is truth. Being submitted to God, and taking responsibility for yourself are good things; they are mature, adult things to do.

What you need to do is get a new heart, a heart that is humble and contrite rather than hard. So how do you get a new heart? Good question. The answer is found in Ezekiel.

Ezekiel 18:31 (NKJV)
"Cast away from you all the transgressions which you have committed, and get yourselves a new heart and a new spirit. For why should you die? O house of Israel?"

You get a new heart by casting away transgressions, by getting rid of your sins and offenses. The only way to do this is to repent. Breaking up your fallow ground is not easy. That is why the lazy farmer did not do it. Even though it isn't easy, it is nonetheless a tough prerequisite to sowing good seed and reaping a great harvest.

Breaking up the fallow ground of your heart involves dying to self and getting rid of the weeds or past sins in your life. As we said earlier, a hard heart is basically a self-centered heart; a heart that has hardened to others and turned inward to self. One of the most difficult things to do is to die to self and admit past wrongs. This is where the rubber meets the road, so to speak. If you are serious about having a good marriage, you have to break up that fallow ground.

A Look at Yourself

Breaking up your fallow ground is difficult because it requires that you take a look at yourself through the eyes of truth. You are not looking at your spouse to see what is wrong with them. You are looking at yourself to see what is in you that cause problems in your relationship. Remember, in Matthew 7:3 & 4, Jesus said we should get the beam out of our own eye before we worry about the spec in someone else's eye.

Ask yourself these questions. Is anyone, especially your spouse, offended with you? Is there something in your marriage you wish had never happened? Do you still remember something in your marriage that you would rather forget? Do you wish you could change anything about your marriage? If the answer to any of these questions is yes, there is probably work for you to do.

Benefits of Breaking up Your Fallow Ground

There are many benefits to breaking up your fallow ground. These benefits are worth the effort, even though it can be a difficult thing to do.

The biggest single benefit is that forgiveness plus repentance equal reconciliation. Let me give you a story to illustrate. When Rebekah got born again, she found out that the only way our relationship could work is if she forgave me of all the offenses that I had committed against her. So she forgave me, but until I admitted that I had done anything wrong, our relationship was not reconciled. As long as I thought I had done nothing wrong,

I could not accept her forgiveness. After all, I felt like she had nothing to forgive me for.

It is the same way with God. Jesus came and took our sins upon Himself and paid the debt for us. He forgave us, but until we admit we had sinned, and repent, we can't be saved. Therefore, we are not in right relationship with God until repentance takes place. I can't be born again if I think I've never sinned - I would think there was nothing for God to forgive me for. Therefore, I would have nothing to repent for. Again, forgiveness alone does not equal reconciliation; you have to bring in repentance too.

When you sin against God and your spouse you must make things right with both in order to totally clear up the offense. You do this by recognizing the offense, confessing it and asking both God and your spouse to forgive you. This is an important step in restoring and maintaining unity in your marriage relationship.

In the previous chapter, you had to recognize unforgiven sins committed against you and forgive the offender. In breaking up fallow ground, you identify sins **you** have committed against others but for which **you** have not repented. Again, this is an important step in restoring your marriage—one that goes even beyond forgiveness. It teaches you to recognize and avoid actions that offend your spouse.

There are also other benefits to breaking up your fallow ground. A boat load of benefits are listed below.

2 Corinthians 7:11 (MSG)
"And now, isn't it wonderful all the ways in which this distress has goaded you closer to God? You're more alive, more concerned, more sensitive, more reverent, more human, more passionate, more responsible. Looked at from any angle, you've come out of this with purity of heart."

The scriptures immediately preceding 2 Corinthians 7:11 show that the distress they were feeling was the act of repentance. Look at all the benefits that resulted from this "distress" of repentance. Who doesn't want to be more alive? It is good to be more concerned for others, more reverent toward God, etc! All of these benefits are signs of other-centeredness and not self-centeredness. Here you can clearly see how repentance really does break up the fallow ground of a hard, selfish heart and give you a new heart.

There are other benefits as well. Repentance clears your conscience which helps you get beyond past failures and do right in the future.

I Timothy 1:19 (CEV)

"You will be faithful and have a clear conscience. Some people have made a mess of their faith because they didn't listen to their consciences."

Repentance results in a clear conscience and not having a clear conscience can mess up your faith, because your heart condemns you. People whose conscience bothers them often feel that they may as well do whatever comes their way. They think, "Well, I lied to my spouse yesterday, I might as well lie again today." Having a clear conscience makes a person less likely to say, "Well, I might as well do this too." Consider also the example of being on a diet. It is common that when people blow their diet in the morning, they will blow it the rest of the day too. They think, "Well I ate that earlier, I might as well eat this too."

The process of breaking up your fallow ground also gives you peace and joy—it makes you feel good about yourself. Hebrews 10:22 (NIV) says we can draw near to God "...with a sincere heart in full assurance of faith, having our hearts sprinkled clean from an evil conscience." If your mind is constantly worried about sins in your past, you will have no peace in your relationship with God.

Before I became a Christian I was a terrible insomniac. I would be dog tired, but the minute my head hit the pillow, my mind would begin to race and I couldn't go to sleep. I would think about all kinds of stuff. What if this happens? What if that happens? What is so-and-so finds out about that? How am I going to pay this bill? I remember one period of 30 days when I never slept more than an hour in any one night. I recall several occasions during that month when I laid in bed and watched the clock tick all the way around until the alarm went off, never having slept a wink. I had anything but a clear conscience. Once I became a born again Christian, and repented of the way I had been living, I have never had insomnia like that again.

Consider this, if you and your spouse have an argument in the morning and you don't clear it up before your day starts, are you as productive? Many people are not. They keep replaying that unresolved argument in their head and it distracts them from accomplishing all that they normally could do if they had not had the argument. Also, if you go to bed angry, you are not likely to sleep as well, and the Bible warns against this.

Finally, breaking up fallow ground and confessing your sins helps you to receive mercy from God and, I believe, from your spouse. This is exemplified in Proverbs.

Proverbs 28:13
"Whoever confesses and forsakes his sins will obtain mercy."

If you confess your sins to someone, and ask for forgiveness, they are much more likely to exercise mercy. I know so. When I offend Rebekah and I go to her and repent, she is much more likely to be merciful and forgive quickly than if I am stubborn and won't admit being wrong. Repenting relaxes the anger the offended person might feel and makes it easier to be merciful. On the other hand, if I am prideful and don't ask for forgiveness, it makes it more difficult for her to extend mercy and forgive me.

Ecclesiastes10:4 in the (AMP)
"For gentleness and calmness prevent or put a stop to great offenses."

It's hard not to come across as kind and gentle when you are asking for forgiveness—provided you are doing it with a right attitude. This attitude, according to the Bible, will put a stop to even great offenses. A lot of married people have great offenses between each other. If your spouse has smoke pouring out of his or her ears, this is how you put a stop to it.

Understanding Repentance

What is repentance? Is it just saying you are sorry? No – it is more than saying you are sorry. Repentance means a change of mind in those who have finally recognized the hurts they have caused and who have decided to pursue a better course of life. This involves recognizing your sin and being genuinely sorry for hurts you have caused. True repentance results in changes in behavior which is expressed by good deeds. Matthew talks about this.

Matthew 3:8 (AMP)
"Bring forth fruit that is consistent with repentance [let your lives prove your change of heart]."

To truly repent means to see your sins, to hate them, and to forsake them. Just being sorry is not enough. You must turn from your sin and do what is right. Repentance involves facing your past sins, confessing them to God and your spouse, and asking for their forgiveness. Everyone makes a mistake. To expect perfection of your spouse or yourself is foolish. However, not being perfect should not be used as an excuse or a cop-out. You should not expect perfection, but you can reasonably expect to see improvement and progress in yourself and in your spouse.

Let's look at 2 Corinthians.

2 Corinthians 7:10 (NKJV)

"For Godly sorrow produces repentance leading to salvation, not to be regretted; but the sorrow of the world produces death."

This scripture is describing two types of sorrow; Godly sorrow and worldly sorrow. Godly sorrow means that you see your sin, you understand the hurt it caused, and you truly regret the hurt it has caused. Because of Godly sorrow, you hate the sin, forsake it, and ask for forgiveness. This is an other-centered view of your sins; you are concerned about the effect your sin has had on others, especially your spouse.

Worldly sorrow means you are sorry that you got caught in your sin, but not necessarily sorry that you committed the sin. When someone gets caught doing something wrong, they have to deal with unpleasant consequences—or "face the music" so to speak. They are very, very sorry to be suffering these consequences. This is a self-centered view of your sins; you are concerned about getting yourself out of a jam. You will typically say you are sorry and apologize profusely for what you did; the purpose of all this is to get the unpleasant consequences to stop. Once you are out of the jam, you will eventually go right back to the same behavior because you never considered or understood how your actions affected your spouse. This type of sorrow will kill your relationship.

2 Corinthians 7:10 also says that Godly sorrow leads to salvation or life. It can certainly help save a marriage. If you can empathize with the pain your sins have caused your spouse, you can better understand how to stop hurting your spouse. The scripture says that worldly sorrow leads to death -- looking out for yourself and being sorry only because you got caught or are facing unpleasant circumstances will undoubtedly kill a marriage.

Here is an example of worldly sorrow that I believe everyone can relate to. Suppose you are doing 70 miles per hour in a 55 mile per hour speed zone, and you see blue lights in your rear view mirror. Worldly sorrow will quickly kick in. You are very sorry that you got caught and you begin apologizing and making excuses. "I didn't realize how fast I was going." "My speedometer must be broken." "I didn't know the speed limit had changed." The officer finishes writing and hands you your ticket or warning, whatever the case may be. He pulls off and you rejoin traffic too. In ten minutes, you are doing 70 in a 55 again. That's worldly sorrow folks; you never repented, you just wanted to get out of the unpleasant circumstances.

I remember when I used to offend Rebekah; I would feel the worldly kind of sorrow. She would get mad at me. I did not like the unpleasant circumstances so I would apologize to get her over being mad. The problem was that I had no real intention of changing my behavior. I would simply resolve to do a better job of not getting caught the next time. Of course, I would get caught sooner or later and soon my apologies became meaningless to Rebekah because she knew I didn't really mean it. I totally lost her trust. This behavior is a nail in the coffin lid of a marriage.

Godly sorrow leads us to true repentance and true repentance is always accompanied by good fruit. As we saw above, Matthew 3:8 says, "Produce fruit in keeping with repentance". If you truly repent of your sins against your spouse, the fruit that will come forth is a better marriage.

Breaking up your fallow ground may not be very pleasant for you, but it does produce very good fruit. Not doing it is the same as giving up on your marriage.

How to Break Up Your Fallow Ground

Notice the title of this section is how to break up YOUR fallow ground. A lot of times people try to break up their spouse's fallow ground. Take it from me, it won't work. You must remember to keep the focus on you or you are likely to make things worse. This process is not easy, but it is a necessary prerequisite to restoring and maintaining unity in your marriage relationship.

The logical question now is, "How do I do this?" We have found the following method to be effective and extremely beneficial to many couples we have worked with over the years. Someone told us that as she and her husband went through this process, and that her heart just melted toward him. She said it was indescribable the sense of release and reconciliation that took place between them. They both told us that they would never want to go back to where they were before.

The first part of this exercise is for you to do alone—NOT with your spouse. Our hope is that you and your spouse are both doing this exercise, but you can do it alone. Read through the whole exercise before doing it so that you will know exactly what to do and how to do it. One word of caution; follow these directions strictly. Deviation could start a counterproductive argument. You'll see what I mean as you read further.

Get a pencil and paper. Pray and ask God to show **you** any offenses **you** have committed against your spouse or others that affects your marriage today. Be honest or contrite—admit to yourself that you are at fault and write the offenses down as God reveals them to you. When you finish this, go back over your list a couple of times, and each time consider the past offenses you have written down and ask God to show you anything that may be missing.

It is important that you prayerfully do this. Many people have done things in their past that do not affect their marriage relationship today; there may be things that happened in your life or in relationships you had before you ever met your spouse. While such things may require repentance before God, it is unlikely that they are offenses against your spouse. Let God lead you.

Is this really necessary? Yes. This is necessary to make sure you clean up everything once and for all. Write specifically what the offense was—do not be general. Confess these offenses to God and ask for His forgiveness.

Next, set a time and place where you can be alone with your spouse without being interrupted. The place and time are very important. Pray that God will prepare both you and your spouse before you do this. Go in with the attitude we talked about in the last chapter. You will forgive anything and everything. This is a good place to exercise the Golden Rule. When you have this time and place, start this part of the exercise. Take your list that you wrote for this exercise with you. Confess to your spouse those offenses you committed against them and ask your spouse's forgiveness.

Here are some important keys to doing this effectively and without causing strife:

- Do not beat around the bush.
- Do not make excuses.
- Do not try to share blame.
- Do not say, "If I offended you..." Accept the responsibility.
- Identify the specific sin and ask forgiveness.
- Be brief - the less words you use, the less likely you are to start an argument.

To help you get started, here is a list of possible sins against your spouse. Do not consider how your spouse may have committed these against you. Consider only what you may have done.

1. Putting things or people (other than God) above your spouse.
2. Materialism.
3. Lying to your spouse.

4. Lack of respect to your spouse. Making them the brunt of a joke, belittling them in front of others.
5. Hypocrisy - asking for forgiveness of offenses you intend to repeat.
6. Uncontrolled anger toward your spouse.
7. Criticism - putting your spouse down in front of others.
8. Complaining and faultfinding.
9. Broken promises.
10. Half-heartedness.
11. Laziness.
12. Ingratitude - not appreciating your spouse's efforts and contributions.
13. Unforgiveness toward your spouse.

Should you confess everything? Good question. As hard as it is, the answer is yes. If you don't confess everything, the devil will make sure you wind up living in fear that your spouse will find out. As we discussed above, your conscience won't be clear, you will lack peace, your mind won't rest, your faith will be hindered, etc. Fear is the devil's playground. Why go there? It is best to confront it, put it behind you, and move on.

This is your opportunity to have a fresh start and a clean slate in your marriage. Here is an example of how to repent to your spouse. "Rebekah, I'm sorry that I have been putting work above you in our relationship. I'm repenting of that and asking you to forgive me."

Here is an example of repenting for something that your spouse may know anything about. "Rebekah, I have been lying to you about working late on Thursdays. I have been watching the game with the guys. I'm sorry I did it, I am repenting of it, and I am asking you to forgive me."

Remember this, repentance means that you turn away from the sin. If you repent and continue with the sin, then you have not repented at all. Luke 3:8 says that we should bring forth fruit in keeping with repentance, and the amplified Bible further adds that a change in our life should prove our change of heart. If you continue in the sin, you have not repented.

Finally, if you are the person being repented to, put James 1:19 into practice. Be "swift to hear, slow to speak, and slow to wrath". Listen to your spouse, keep your mouth shut, and don't get mad! Forgive!! This is for the good of your marriage; don't ruin it by not allowing them to repent. Remember—in the last chapter, you made a "big decision" to forgive every sin!

At the end of the last chapter, I noted that forgiveness alone does not equal reconciliation and restoration. Forgiveness plus true repentance does equal reconciliation and restoration. The two together close the loop and restore unity.

A Final Note about Forgiveness and Repentance

Sometimes people find forgiving and repenting to be too hard. They just can't bring themselves to forgive someone who has hurt them so much. Or maybe they just can't repent to this person because, after all, they were in the wrong too; they hurt me, and I don't want to apologize for what I did after all that they did to me.

No matter how hard it may seem, you can do it. In fact, God says you can. Look at 2 Corinthians.

2 Corinthians 5:18 & 19 (NKJV)
"Now all things are of God, who has reconciled us to Himself through Jesus Christ, and has given us the ministry of reconciliation, that is, that God was in Christ reconciling the world to Himself, not imputing their trespasses to them, and has committed to us the word of reconciliation."

God has called you to the ministry of reconciliation. If he has called you, he has anointed you. You can do it!

Chapter 4

A MORE EXCELLENT WAY

WHEN Rebekah and I first got married, one of the biggest obstacles in our relationship was that I did not know how to love her. Knowing how to love someone tends to be something that people take for granted. We just expect it to come naturally, but it doesn't.

In my case I did love Rebekah. Sometimes when we were fighting, or money was tight, or things just weren't going my way, I would question my love for her. During these times I'd think, "Maybe this marriage is a mistake. Maybe we shouldn't have gotten married." But when I looked deep down inside, I knew that I did love her.

The fact that I felt that I loved Rebekah did not automatically mean that she felt love from me. In other words, my feelings of love did not translate into outward signs of love that she could see. Even though I would tell Rebekah that I loved her, it was not enough to convince her. She felt like it was just empty talk. Love is something that can be seen—the following scriptures say so.

2 Corinthians 8:24 (CEV)
"Treat them in such a way that the churches will see your love and will know why we bragged about you."

1 John 3:18 (NLT)

"Dear children, let us stop just saying we love each other; let us really show it by our actions."

I felt love for Rebekah and told her that I loved her, but my actions were not saying "I love you" Obviously these scriptures show that there is more to love than feelings and words; your actions must show your love as well. True love can be seen.

Our everyday language even reflects this in common phrases that we all say. Everyone reading this has heard phrases like these.

- "Talk is cheap."
- "Put your money where your mouth is."
- "Actions speak louder than words."

All of these clichés are talking about backing your words up with your actions. The reason Rebekah didn't feel that I loved her anymore was because there was no action backing up my words. When Rebekah and I were dating, she held a higher priority in my life. My actions proved that. I spent a lot of time with her, I took time off work to be with her, I spent money on her, and she knew I thought about her because I would call her up on the telephone. My life tended to center more around her.

However, later on my career became the most important thing in my life. I gave all of my time, my thoughts, and my energy to it, and when I did have time off it was spent watching football, reading, or doing some other activity alone. I thought she should feel love from me in spite of this. I told her I loved her, but the words became empty to her because there were no actions backing them up.

I was not able to love Rebekah in a way that she could understand – in a way that she would interpret as love. So, what I needed to do was learn how to demonstrate my love for Rebekah. I needed to learn to make my actions confirm what I felt and what I said. To do that, I needed an example to follow. I needed someone to show me and teach me how to do it. But who?

God Teaches Us to Love

The Bible says, "Seek and you shall find" (Matthew 7:7). It is amazing how when you are looking for something; God will help you find the answers. Soon after realizing I needed help learning to love Rebekah, I came across the following scripture.

1 Thessalonians 4:9b (KJV)
"...For ye yourselves are taught of God to love one another."

God will teach you how to love other people; God taught me how to love my spouse and He will teach you how to love your spouse too! When I saw this I said, "OK, there it is; God's love is perfect, and He is willing to teach me to love others." I figured I could not possibly do any better than having God Himself teach me how to love Rebekah. So I started studying what the Bible says about love, praying about love, and asking God to teach me how to love Rebekah.

Some people think that they can't possibly learn something like this from the Bible. They want some brilliant counselor with a lot of degrees and research statistics to help them learn it. Rebekah and I thought this way too. But the brilliant counselor, a Ph.D. Psychologist, told us we were hopeless and should get a divorce. The things that God taught us are what saved our marriage, and those same things continue to help our marriage grow today.

Whose Way?

Some people think you should love your spouse their way rather than your way. To love your spouse their way means that you put their needs, wants and desires above your own and love them the way they want to be loved. This sounds right, but it's not quite right. If you love them your way, you put your needs wants and desires above theirs and you wind up loving them the way you think they should be loved rather than how they want to be loved.

So loving your spouse their way certainly seems like a good idea. But consider this example. Suppose you have a typical small child. If you love them their way, attempting to meet all their needs, wants and desires, you'll feed them chocolate, cookies, ice cream, and soda instead of broccoli, chicken, milk and peas. You'll let them play all the time instead of giving them chores to teach them responsibility. You'll let them stay up late and watch whatever they wanted on television. You'll even let them go off with a stranger if they wanted to all in the name of loving them their way—trying to serve their needs, wants, and desires.

Obviously, you can't love a child their way simply because many of their desires are self-centered. You have to temper loving them their way with your greater knowledge concerning what is best for them.

In the same way, you can't just love your spouse their way. All of us have wants and desires that may be self-centered and dictated by our flesh. Some of these desires may not line up with God's will for us. Meeting these wants and desires would not be good for anyone, and may even lead us to sin.

For example, suppose your spouse wants a new TV, but your budget just won't stretch that far right now. You may be tempted to steal in order to get the means to buy the TV. If you give in to this temptation, you'll meet your spouse's short-term desire for the TV, but you have sinned by stealing. Here again, you see that loving your spouse their way must be tempered by greater knowledge, and the greater knowledge in this case needs to come from God. Thus you must love your spouse God's way and not their way or your way. This is consistent with scripture.

John 13:34 (KJV)
"A new commandment I give unto you, that ye love one another, as I have loved you, that ye also love one another."

Here Jesus clearly commands that we are to love one another (and one another includes your spouse) as He loved us. He is saying love them My way, not their way and not your way. Again, in Ephesians we find this instruction.

Ephesians 5:25 (KJV)
"Husbands, love your wives as Christ also loved the church, and gave Himself for it."

This scripture specifically addresses marriage and says the husband is to love the wife God's way. There can be no doubt that you must love your spouse God's way. It all comes back to letting God teach you to love your spouse. Keep in mind that love is something that you grow in. None of us will ever be all the way there. The rest of this chapter is devoted to helping you learn how to love your spouse God's way.

The Characteristics of God's Love

You can't love your spouse God's way unless you understand the characteristics of God's love. What does His love look like? There are some key Scriptures that describe what His love looks like. Let's take a look at them.

Romans 8:35-39 (KJV)
"Who shall separate us from the love of Christ? Shall tribulation, or distress, or persecution, or famine, or nakedness, or peril, or sword?

As it is written, "For thy sake we are killed all the day long; we are accounted as sheep for the slaughter. Nay, in all these things we are more than conquerors through Him that loved us. For I am persuaded, that neither death, nor life, nor angels, nor principalities, nor powers, nor things present, nor things to come, nor height, nor depth, nor any other creature, shall be able to separate us from the love of God, which is in Christ Jesus our Lord."

From this scripture we see that nothing can separate us from God's love. Think about it. Even we can't separate ourselves from His love. No matter what we do, He loves us—even if we don't love him. His love, in other words, is totally unconditional. There are no strings attached; there are no tricks up His sleeve.

John 15:13 (KJV)
"Greater love hath no man than this, that a man lay down his life for his friends."

Here we see that God's love is sacrificial. This scripture isn't just talking about dying for someone. It is talking about laying down your needs and wants and desires to meet those of others. Jesus always put Himself last. In every situation, He sacrificed His own comfort, time, rights, and so on for others.

Jeremiah 31:3 (KJV)
"The Lord hath appeared of old unto me, saying, Yea, I have loved thee with an everlasting love: therefore with loving-kindness have I drawn thee."

From this scripture we see that God's love for us is everlasting. He does not get tired of loving us no matter how unlovable we might be. Think of what that means! Imagine the worst person you can— Hitler or Osama Bin Laden. God loves them anyway, with an everlasting love.

Taken together, these scriptures tell us that God's love is unconditional, sacrificial, and everlasting. That is the kind of love we must have for our spouse.

Let Me Count the Ways

You may have noticed that I have been referring to God's kind of love. To say that there is a God kind of love implies that there are other kinds of love. In the English language we have one word for love and that is the word "love". As you may know, the New Testament was originally written in ancient Greek. The ancient Greeks had three basic words describing three different types of love. Let's take a look at those. Understanding the different types of love will give you a better framework for understanding God's love.

One Greek word for love is Eros. Eros basically means lust. It is a wanton type of love that derives from the sexual drive of a person. One dictionary defines it as love directed toward self-realization. So basically, eros is a love that seeks to meet the needs or desires of self—no concern for the needs or desires of others is contemplated in this word. Eros depends on the circumstances of the moment to exist. If a couple is in the middle of passion, it can thrive. When the passion is fulfilled, it disappears. There is no lasting quality and no commitment with eros. The word eros does not appear in the New Testament. Since it does not appear in the New Testament you can safely bet that eros has nothing whatsoever to do with God's love.

A second Greek word for love is phileo. Phileo means brotherly love or to be a friend to someone. Philadelphia, the "City of Brotherly Love" gets its name from this word. The word phileo implies sentiment or feeling. This type of love is chiefly a matter of the heart. When most people say, "I love you," this is what they mean; they are saying they have a feeling for you. Phileo is used 19 times in the New Testament.

The third Greek word for love is agape. Agape is defined in The Eerdmans Bible Dictionary as a "divine, selfless love which will go to any length to attain the wellbeing of its object." This type of love implies a decision and a commitment. It is a matter of the head more than of the heart - it is not based on feelings. It involves judgment and the deliberate assent of the will. Agape implies action. People must choose to exercise it. This is the word for love used in all of the scriptures we have looked at thus far (except in Jeremiah 31:3. In that scripture the word used for love is "hesed" which is the Hebrew equivalent of agape found in the New Testament). John 3:16 tells us that it was this type of love that motivated God to restore His relationship with man. Agape appears over 150 times in the New Testament. Agape is the primary type of love as far as God is concerned.

Agape love means not being self-centered. To the extent you are being self-centered; you are not walking in love. Love and self-centeredness exclude each other—they cannot exist together.

Galatians 5:13 (AMP)
"For you, brethren, were [indeed] called to freedom; only [do not let your] freedom be an incentive to your flesh and an opportunity or excuse [for selfishness], but through love you should serve one another."

This scripture contrasts two opposites—selfishness and love. Did you get that? Selfishness is the opposite of love. You cannot love and be selfish at the same time! This scripture encourages us not to be selfish, but to love instead. You see, true love serves others—it does not serve self.

Me? Do This in My Marriage?

At this point you might be starting to think, "But I can't do this!!" Or maybe, "But this is God's love - divine love. That doesn't apply to me and my marriage." Well—have I got good news for you! It does apply in your marriage, and you can do it. Let's look at John 13:34 (KJV).

John 13:34 (KJV)
"A new commandment I give unto you, that ye love one another; as I have loved you, that ye also love one another."

Here Jesus commands us to love one another as He has loved us. The word that Jesus uses here is agape. Clearly, we are to love each other with agape love—that includes your spouse. Now let's look at a scripture from Ephesians.

Ephesians 5:25 (KJV)
"Husbands, love your wives, even as Christ also loved the church, and gave Himself for it."

Here we find that husbands are to love, or agape, their wives as Christ loved the church. There is no getting around it. You are supposed to love your spouse unselfishly, and with this agape type of love.

Now, let's make sure one thing is clear. Just because Ephesians says "husbands love your wives as Christ loved the Church" does not mean that wives do not have to love their husbands this way. Remember John 13:34 said we are to love "one another" with agape love. So this means wives as well as husbands.

Note that these scriptures, including John 13:34, are stated as commands. The requirement to love others is not optional—it is not a suggestion. It is a command. In fact I have heard the law of love called "THE" New Testament command. Therefore, agape love is applicable to your marriage. God expects you to love your spouse this way. And remember this, Philippians 4:13 says that we can do all things through Christ who strengthens us!!!

The Benefits of Agape Love

Exercising agape love in your marriage relationship will result in many benefits. For example, if you love your spouse with agape love, there is no room left for the word "divorce" in your relationship. It has to go. Agape, remember, is not based on a feeling. Let's look at the meaning of this word again. Agape is a divine, selfless love which will go to any length to attain the wellbeing of its object. This type of love implies a decision and a commitment. It is a matter of the head more than of the heart—it is not based on feelings. It involves judgment and the deliberate assent of the will.

In Matthew 19:6 (NIV), Jesus said, speaking of marriage, "What God has joined together, let man not separate." God wants you to be committed to the wellbeing of your marriage relationship just as He is committed to the wellbeing of His relationship with mankind. When you know that your spouse is absolutely committed to you, a feeling of great security comes into your marriage relationship. The commitment required to bring this security is spelled a-g-a-p-e.

Another benefit of agape love is found in 1 John.

1 John 4:18 (NKJV)

"There is no fear in love; but perfect love casts out fear, because fear involves torment. But he who fears has not been made perfect in love."

Perfect love, agape love, drives out fear. As you love your spouse with agape love, their fears are driven out. They begin to feel peace in the marriage relationship and their trust in you grows. As this happens, and their fear subsides, they become more able to love you. Fear hinders love and other-centeredness. People don't want to trust because they are afraid their trust will be betrayed.

By loving your spouse with this committed, unconditional, agape love, you can actually help your spouse love you with this same kind of committed, unconditional, agape love. That last statement is as important as anything you will read in this book.

Now, and this point is very important too, as you and your spouse grow in your relationship with the Lord, and begin to understand and accept His agape love, you both will be able to believe His promises, and put your faith in Him to greater and greater extents. Galatians 5:6 in the Amplified Bible says that our faith is "...activated and energized and expressed and working by love." Here is another huge benefit of agape love. As your love grows, your faith grows. Think of what that will mean to your marriage and all other aspects of life such as prosperity, health, and happiness!

That is what 1 John 4:18 is talking about. Agape love drives out fear. It causes you to have faith and trust in the giver of the love. As this grows it enables the person receiving the love to become other-centered. This causes them to return the agape love to their spouse. As I consistently give agape love to Rebekah, her trust in me grows and in that way I am actually able to help her love me with agape love.

The same is true with God. As we come to understand His love, we are more able to believe, trust, and have faith in Him. Because we have faith in Him, we are not operating out of fear, and we make decisions based on His love for us. These decisions are other-centered decisions that involve putting others, including your spouse, first and trusting God to take care of our needs.

Still another benefit of agape love is found in 1 Peter.

1 Peter 4:8 (AMP)
"...for love covers a multitude of sins [forgives and disregards the offenses of others]."

There is an old saying that says, "Love is blind but marriage is a real eye opener." There is a lot of truth in this. It seems that during courtship, when we are intent on the "prize" rather than on ourselves, we overlook any and all flaws. After the wedding, the focus tends to shift more toward ourselves again, and low-and-behold, our eyes are opened to all of the flaws of our spouse. If you have a spouse that never snapped at you or got angry with you until after you were married, this is why.

During your courtship, they were focusing on you and your needs. After the marriage, their attention went to themselves and their needs. But, even if your spouse is acting this way, that does not give you an excuse to do the same. You need to focus on walking in love toward them.

When we love someone, really love them, it is easy to overlook their faults. Looking at someone through the eyes of love is kind of like looking backwards through a pair of binoculars. When you look through binoculars the right way, everything is magnified. If there are any flaws, you can see them more clearly; they seem bigger than they really are. But, if you look through the wrong end of binoculars— look in the big end and out the small end—whatever you are looking at looks very small. The flaws are small and easy to overlook. This is true with love. If we love someone, their faults and mistakes look small and insignificant.

A lot of people have trouble with this. It seems that we often demand a higher level of perfection from our spouse than from anyone else. Even small mistakes can seem inexcusable when it is our spouse making them. Loving our spouse with agape love helps us deal with these things in a much better way. It helps us to keep a right perspective when we make mistakes.

Also with agape love comes unconditional acceptance. God accepts and loves each of us just as we are. As we grow in the knowledge of this love, and because He loves us this way, it changes our attitude about ourselves, and causes us to change our attitudes about our behavior. We actually want to improve. The same is true when we love our spouse unconditionally. It causes them to start reacting to us differently. It will cause their attitude to change also. To withhold love because you don't like your spouse's habits or behavior or how they act is contrary to God's will and the command to love one another. Love them unconditionally and continue to grow in love toward them. This, of course, goes for both partners in the marriage relationship. But usually, one starts first. Grow in love—self-sacrificing, agape love—toward your spouse.

Finally, there is a lot of talk about excellence these days. Everyone wants excellence in their marriage, excellence in their ministry, excellence in business, and excellence in education. 1 Corinthians 12:31 (NKJV) says, "...and yet I show you a more excellent way", and then proceeds into an in- depth discussion of walking in love. Love is excellence; the two cannot be separated. If you want excellence in any or all areas of life, you need to grow in love.

To summarize, agape love has so many benefits. It brings security to relationships. It drives out fear. It is critical to walking in faith. It covers over your sins and offenses. It accepts you unconditionally. It will lead to excellence in life. Frankly, your success in life, in any area, will be limited if you do not walk in agape love.

Again, you might be thinking there is no way that you can love anyone like this. But if you think about it, there is at least one person that we all love with agape love. When that person makes a mistake or sins, we know that they meant the best and we are quick to forgive them. We know they aren't such a bad person. We tend to think the best of them in every situation. You judge this person by their intentions instead of their actions. Their flaws seem small and insignificant. Who am I talking about? Who is this person we all love in this way? It is **yourself!** When Jesus said "love your neighbor as yourself," this is what he was referring to.

Feelings

Many people think that love is a feeling; I used to think this way. Back when I first became a Christian, people would sometimes come up to me and say things like, "Don't you just love the Lord?" I would lie to them and say, "Why, yes, of course I do!" I'd think to myself, "I don't feel love for God, but I am not going to tell these church folks that. I knew I was supposed to love God, and I wanted to feel love, but I just didn't seem to feel like they did. I thought love was a feeling. I didn't know what love was. Now, I know that I did love God. I just didn't know it at the time. The key is that love is not a feeling.

When Rebekah and I talk to people, they often tell us that they no longer feel love for their spouse. That sentimental or passionate feeling they associate with love is gone, and they don't know how to get it back, or even if it is possible to get the feeling back. A lot of people want their marriage to work, but they think it's hopeless if they don't feel love for their spouse anymore. You can get it back! The Word of God tells you how in 1 Thessalonians.

1 Thessalonians 4:9 (AMP)
"But concerning brotherly love (for all other Christians), you have no need to have any one write you, for you yourselves have been (personally) taught by God to love one another."

To understand how this scripture applies, you need to know that the first time the word love is used in this scripture, it is the Greek word phileo. The second time the word love is used it is the Greek word agape. So what the writer is telling us is that you don't need to be taught how to have a feeling type of love because God has taught you how to have the committed, self-sacrificing type of love. In other words, feelings will follow a decision.

I used to run three miles a day for exercise when I was in the military. I don't recall ever feeling like going running. I looked at it as a chore. It was something I had committed to do to stay in shape. Let me describe a typical day's run to you. Every day after work, I would put on my running clothes and drive real slowly out to the running track. I'd slowly get out of the car, and slowly walk to the track. Then, when the excuses were over, I'd start running. About one-half to three-quarters of a mile into my run, a strange thing would happen. I would start getting into the rhythm, and I would actually begin to feel like running. For the next two plus miles, I felt like running. You see, feelings follow a decision. If the love is gone in your marriage, make a decision to love your spouse with agape love, and the feelings will return.

This is very true in my relationship with Rebekah. As I said earlier there were times in the past when we did not feel love for each other. Now, however, after applying agape love to our relationship, we can say that we have both a strong commitment **and** a strong feeling of love for each other. From the agape love flowed the phileo love. The feelings we wanted came back!!! The same can be true for you. If you don't feel love for your spouse, I challenge you to try this. It will work for you just like it did for us.

Don't rely on your feelings. Feelings will lie to you. The below scripture from Jeremiah explains further.

Jeremiah17:9 (AMP)
"The heart is deceitful above all things, and it is exceedingly perverse and corrupt and severely, mortally sick! Who can know it [perceive, understand, be acquainted with his own heart and mind]?"

The word for heart used here is the Hebrew word "leb." Leb means the seat of the emotions and passions. It also refers to your mind and your will. Your emotions, or feelings, can't be trusted. They will tell you that you love someone when you just feel lust. They might even tell you that you don't love someone when you do, or that marriage was a mistake. Don't be led by them. Be led by the Bible.

Let me give you an example. Airplane pilots can be visually or instrument certified. An instrument certified pilot can fly the plane safely when visibility is bad. He can fly in rain, snow, fog, darkness, etc. Even in bad conditions, he can keep his eyes on the instruments and safely finish his flight. A pilot that is visually certified must be able to see the horizon to safely fly the plane. If he can't see the horizon, he can easily get disoriented and think the plane is flying up when it is actually diving into the ground.

Here is the comparison. The pilot who is visually certified is like someone who is led by their emotions or feelings. They may listen to their feelings and think I don't love my spouse anymore, the thrill is gone. This circumstance can obscure their vision causing them to get disoriented and cause them to wreck their life. The whole time they think they are doing the right thing by being led by their feelings. On the other hand, the instrument certified pilot is like a person who is guided by the Word of God. Even when difficult circumstances come, or his or her feelings change, they let the Word of God guide them, not their feelings. Pretty soon their feelings are back in line, and things are great. All this person had to do to safely "fly" was keep on doing the Word.

If you allow yourself to be led by your feelings you are setting yourself up to be led by the devil. In John 14:30 and 2 Corinthians 4:3 the Bible makes it clear that the devil rules this world. Because of that, he has some ability to devise circumstances that will affect your feelings. The devil's job is to kill, steal, and destroy (see John 10:10). You can be sure that any circumstances he sets up will lead to death and destruction. Fly by the instruments of God's Word and do not be led by feelings!

How to Take the Excellent Path

I think all of us who want a better life, better relationships, and more happiness, would want to take the excellent path. "How do I do this? How do I take this path and love my spouse the agape way?" Let me assure you that it is possible. There is a saying that goes, "What God appoints He anoints." God appointed (or commanded) you to love your spouse with agape love. He will not call you to do anything without equipping you to do it. Therefore, you are able to do this.

To enjoy all of the benefits of love, you have to know how to grow in love, or, as some people put it, how to "walk in love." Let's look at how you can learn to do that.

It is important to understand that love is something you grow in. No one ever really arrives. No one is ever "all grown up" when it comes to love. The day you think you have perfected your love walk is the day you lost the battle.

Philippians 1:9 (NKJV)
 "And this I pray, that your love may abound still more and more in knowledge and all discernment."

The scripture is clear. Love is something that we should continually grow in.

It is also important to understand that walking in love means consistently giving yourself to others. Ephesians tells us that Jesus, our example in everything, walked in love by giving Himself to others.

Ephesians 5:2 (NKJV)
 "And walk in love, as Christ also has loved us and given Himself for us, an offering and a sacrifice to God for a sweet-smelling aroma."

This giving isn't just talking about going to the cross and dying for our sins. It means putting other people first and serving their needs on a day-in, day-out basis.

Earlier in this chapter when we were defining the Greek words for love, you may have noticed that phileo is a matter of the heart and agape is a matter of the head. This simply means that agape love is a decision and not a feeling. Feelings do result from agape love, but agape love is not based on feelings. Agape love is not dependent on how you might feel, how your day is going, whether someone better looking comes along, if the kids are behaving badly, if your spouse snores, or if you have lots of money or not, or on anything else. You need to make a big decision—a deliberate assent of your will—that you will love your spouse sacrificially and will go to any length, before God, to attain their wellbeing. I say "before God" because whatever you do to attain your spouse's well-being must be in accordance with God's will. Always keep Him first. I will not rob a bank for Rebekah. I have to always keep God first.

Love is a decision!

Colossians 3:14 (NKJV)
  "But above all these things put on love, which is the bond of perfection."

Here we are told to put on love. How many of you stand in front of your closet and your clothes jump on your body? You have to decide what you are going to wear, and put your clothes on yourself. The same is true with love. It is like a garment that we have to decide to put on. Notice that the Bible says to put love on above all things. That tells me that it needs to be the outermost garment that we wear around. No matter what, others should be able to see our love. It should cover everything we do. It was this very thing that proved to me that God was real. It is described in detail in the last chapter of this book, but in brief, Rebekah got me to go to church with her one Sunday because we made a deal. (I wanted her to go somewhere with me, and in turn I had to go to church with her.) I could "see" the love of God on those people there. I knew they couldn't be faking it. The only possibility was that God was real; I knew that was the only way these people could love each other the way that I was seeing. Jesus said, in John 13:35, that people will know you are His disciples by your love for one another.

Something else you need to know is this. When I told Rebekah that divorce was no longer an option, our relationship took a dramatic turn. We were nowhere close to having everything worked out, nor were we getting along really great, but I had made a decision. Divorce was no longer in my vocabulary. I told her I was committed to her no matter how much we fought. This changed Rebekah.

She had been totally insecure before in our relationship, and because I was really committed to her for the first time ever, she was able to begin to trust me. This alone eliminated a lot of fighting because she knew when she woke up the next day, I'd still be there. When there's no commitment in a relationship, it causes a lot of insecurity and lots of arguments. This is true even if you are married. As long as divorce is an option, there is really no commitment. Insecurity causes you to be jealous, suspicious, and irritated. Once commitment and security are established in your relationship, a lot of things you used to fight about no longer matter and you have a lot less trouble.

When you make this decision, you begin to change your thinking. Your thinking must line up with God's Word before your actions will line up with God's Word. If your thinking is wrong, what you believe will be wrong. If your believing is wrong, what you say will be wrong, and you will have actions accordingly. Let me give you an example.

When Rebekah and I dated, we each thought the other one was nice. Therefore, we went out a second time. Each time seemed to be nicer than the first. Pretty soon, we were thinking the other one was pretty great. We even said things like that to each other and other people. We thought about how nice it was to be together. We each individually had these thoughts, and said these words, sometimes to each other, sometimes to other people. We began to have feelings for one another, good feelings. We enjoyed each other; we had feelings of fondness, and eventually love.

Likewise, later in the relationship, as things changed, I acted differently toward Rebekah, she wondered what was wrong. At first she chose to think I was going through an adjustment period with the new job. However, she still thought good things. But after time went by and my behavior didn't change, her thoughts soon changed about me. She began to think, and then began to believe that I didn't feel the same—that I didn't love her anymore. After a while she began to say that I didn't love her, and then her actions began changing too, just like mine did. You might notice that Rebekah thought, then believed, then spoke, and then acted. This is common in relationships. It wasn't just something weird about us. The Bible bears this out. Consider the following scripture.

Proverbs 18:21 (NKJV)
 "Death and life are in the power of the tongue. And those who love it will eat its fruit."

If you think something long enough, it will turn into a belief, and what you believe will be in your heart in abundance. It will come out of your mouth and affect what you do—it will affect your actions.

Matthew 12: 34 – 35 (NKJV)
 "Brood of vipers! How can you being evil, speak good things? For out of the abundance of the heart the mouth speaks. A good man out of the

good treasure of his heart brings forth good things, and an evil man
out of evil treasure brings forth evil things."

Mark 11:23 (NKJV)
"For assuredly, I say to you whoever <u>says</u> to this mountain, 'Be removed
and be cast into the sea,' and does not doubt in his heart, but believes
that those things he <u>says</u> will be done, he will have whatever he says."

You need to begin to say things like, "I love my spouse as
Christ loved the Church." And you need to begin consciously to seek
to attain their well-being. After you say it and do it enough, it will
become second nature. This means your thinking is changing, and
your actions will change for the better too. Your actions will
become more natural rather than forced. You will feel like doing
those things for your spouse. Remember, feelings follow a decision.

We looked at Jeremiah 31:3 earlier. This scripture says God
draws us by his loving kindness. Loving-kindnesses are the acts of
love we do for someone just because we love them. In Hosea 2,
God says He will allure His people and describes the acts of love
He will use to do it. It is interesting that He compares the relationship
to a husband and wife.

In 1 Corinthians 13:12, the Bible says that God fully knows
us. Since God fully knows us, He knows what acts of loving
kindness will draw us to Him. 1 Peter 3 says we are to live with our
wives according to knowledge. In other words, you can only
effectively love our spouse with agape love to the extent that you
know them. Unless you know your spouse intimately, you will wind
up doing what you think is right. You will wind up loving them self-
centeredly, even though that may not be your intent. In this situation,
you are saying "I love you" your way and not God's way.

The closer that you get to God, the better you get to know
Him. As you get to know Him better, you realize that there is so

much more to learn about Him. The same is true with your spouse. It should be a danger sign if we begin to think we "have arrived". What this really means is that you have gotten complacent and are beginning to fall back. If you are working on your relationship, you will realize that you are never all the way there—there will always be room to grow. At first it may seem difficult, but as you keep it up, your feelings line up, and it is a wonderful thing. Think back on how it was when you first fell in love; you did not dread spending time with them then, did you? In fact, you looked forward to it. It can be like that again. God wants you to have great and enjoyable marriage.

Finally, part of walking in love is not keeping score. 1 Corinthians 13:5 (AMP) says that love "takes no account of the evil done to it [it pays no attention to a suffered wrong]." Rebekah and I used to get into fights, and we would both start listing all of the things the other one had done wrong. "Well I'm mad because you don't treat me right. You did this and this and this. And when we were dating you did that and the other, etc." Maybe you have done this too. Do you know what this is? It is keeping a record of the wrongs done to you. Love doesn't do that. Keeping a record of wrongs is the same as dragging all your baggage from the past around with you. When the baggage is bad or no longer wanted, you need to get rid of it. Keeping a record of wrongs creates an atmosphere of hopelessness in a relationship. Your spouse will feel like they can never overcome the past, and then the next step in their thinking will be, "Why try?" You can give them hope by not keeping a record of wrongs.

A Final Word on Love

An old song tells us that love is a many-splendid thing. I agree. Think about all you have read in this chapter, and think about the preceding chapters. If someone is walking in love they will not be self-centered. If someone is walking in love, they will forgive the offenses of others. If someone is walking in love, they will repent when they offend others. In Galatians 5:23 (NKJV), right after listing the fruit of the Spirit (which is the fruit of walking in love) the Bible says, "against such there is no law." To the extent that you walk in love, your spouse will find no fault with you. On the other hand, to the extent you are walking in love, you will find no fault in your spouse. Isn't love grand?

Chapter 5

COVENANT

MOST everyone has heard the marriage relationship referred to as a "covenant relationship", but many people don't fully understand what that means. I have heard people describe a covenant as a type of contract. This is only partly correct; it helps many of us in western culture (America, Europe, Australia, etc.) to understand the concept of a covenant. We live in contract-oriented societies, so we tend to understand what a contract is. A contract can help you understand a covenant to the extent that both are types of agreements under which both parties have responsibilities, but that is about it. In fact, there are more differences between contracts and covenants than there are similarities.

Christians, especially married Christians, need to have an understanding of covenant because the marriage relationship is a covenant relationship. To understand the marriage covenant, you need to understand the Biblical perspective of covenants. In the Bible, covenants are serious business to God. Since they are serious to God, they ought to be serious to us too.

A covenant is similar to a contract, but there are some huge differences as shown below.

Contract	Covenant
In a contract, each party maintains their distinct identity. Goods and/or services are exchanged.	In a covenant, the two parties become one entity. People give themselves.
A contract is based on distrust. The contract is written to protect the parties' assets.	A covenant is based on trust between parties. The assets and liabilities of each party now belong to the other.
A contract is written to define the limits of each party's responsibilities and to limit their liability. It puts limitations on what they have to do to fulfill the agreement.	A covenant is based on unlimited responsibility and liability. Even if one party does not perform, the other party is still responsible to fulfill all of the obligations.
A contract can be voided by mutual consent, if one party fails to perform, or if circumstances change.	A covenant cannot be broken if new circumstances occur (sickness or health, richer or poorer). A covenant only ends when one of the covenant partners dies.
Compromise is common in contracts.	Compromise is not a covenant concept. Each covenant partner gives whatever is required to succeed.
Contracts involve promises (if you do this, I'll do this).	Covenants involve oaths (I'll do my part no matter what you do).
In contracts, you strike a bargain	In covenants, you give all

Covenant is an alien idea to our culture. The simplest way I can describe it is to say that a covenant is an agreement under which two people become one; everything you are and have belongs to and becomes a part of whoever you go into covenant with. For example, suppose I go into covenant with Bill. Bill has a nice ski boat. After entering into covenant with him, I would actually have the right to go over to Bill's house and say, "Bill, I'm taking our boat out for the day!" Likewise, if Bill owes a debt, after entering into the covenant, that debt now belongs to both Bill and me. Bill could rightly say, "Since we're in covenant now, I'll go pay off our debt with our money!" As you can see, it is very important to carefully choose who you enter into covenant with since their assets, liabilities, problems —everything, both good and bad—will now be yours. If you don't want to give away ownership of your ski boat, you better not go into covenant with someone. If you don't want their debts to become yours, don't go into covenant with them. You need to be aware of whom you are going into covenant with; this includes the person you are marrying.

God is a covenant God. Covenant is what the Old and New Testament of the Bible is based on. The word "testament" is simply another word for covenant. The Old Testament describes the Old covenant established with Abraham, and the New Testament describes the New Covenant established with Jesus. Because man kept breaking the Old Covenant (Old Testament), man was separated from God. God wanted His relationship with man restored so much that He sent Jesus to fulfill the law, and take the sins of mankind on Himself so that He could make a better covenant for us based on better promises. Did you know that since man could not keep the covenant, Jesus came?

God knew Jesus would not break the covenant and that we would break it. Therefore, it isn't based on what we did; we have the New Covenant because of what Jesus did. We can't break it, because it's between God and Jesus. We get to partake of it, but we, even when we sin, can't break it. We lose fellowship when we sin, but the covenant is never broken because Jesus paid the price for it.

Even ancient peoples took covenants very seriously. They never entered into a covenant lightly and they never, ever broke covenant. Breaking covenant would actually give others the right to kill you; because of this you would be willing to put everything you had into ensuring that the covenant was upheld. Again, a contract and a covenant are both a form of agreement, but that is where the similarities end!

When you entered into the marriage covenant, all of the assets, liabilities, responsibilities, and problems, of your spouse became yours and vice-versa. Your responsibility to your spouse is unlimited. The covenant cannot be broken because new circumstances come up or if someone better comes along. It's the same type of relationship Jesus has with God. It's a spiritual thing, far above a physical thing. It's the most serious relationship after God you could ever have.

There is a word that describes how you relate to someone in a covenant relationship. It's the Hebrew word "hesed". This word carries lots of meaning that defines how covenant partners are to treat each other; in other words, it describes how you are to treat your spouse. As noted, hesed is a Hebrew word and appears in the Old Testament; it has a counterpart in the New Testament though – the word agape. Hesed is covenant love. It is a steady, loyal, persistent, pursuing, abundant, profuse, unreserved, passionate love. It is the love of God." Remember, the marriage relationship is a covenant, and this is the kind of love we should have for our covenant partner.

Here are some of the concepts included in hesed. This word contains a lot of meaning. It includes the idea that you constantly think about your covenant partner, that you favor them above others, that you behave as if they were with you always, that your covenant commitment is still as fresh today as when it was made it, that you will serve their needs with your all, that you never forget that you are one, and that you go out of your way to bless your covenant partner.

Hesed describes how covenant partners are to treat each other. Think about what was just described above. This is how you fall in love with someone. In fact, we often start out like this. At the beginning we are headed in the right direction. In the "getting to know you" process, dating or courting, we want to bless each other and help each other. Your betrothed is always on your mind. Think about it—that's how we act even before we are in covenant. Shouldn't it just get better afterward?

Often times, it's only during the "pre-covenant" phase that we treat each other right. During this time we make it a priority to get to know each other, so we make time to talk to each other. We grow closer as time goes by, we continue to talk and pursue one another. Our priority is clear; the other person becomes the "significant other" or number one in our life. Sometimes after we get married this changes. The fact is, in order for this to remain true - for your spouse to remain number one—we have to do hesed in our marriage relationship.

It's just like our relationship with God, we cannot grow or even stay where we are with Him if we do not make time for Him, pursue Him, talk to Him, spend time with Him. Remember, we're in covenant with God, it's not a part time thing, or only to be recalled when we need something. It's a covenant just like our marriage relationship.

Here's something to think on. If you are married, you are in covenant, and the two of you are one. If you keep secrets from your spouse, you have broken covenant with them. A secret means concealed from general knowledge or kept hidden. Anything you conceal or keep hidden is a secret. It doesn't matter if it's big or little. I'm not talking about Christmas presents. You know if you're trying to keep something from your spouse, or just trying to keep them generally uninformed. There should be no hidden area, otherwise, trust is broken. How can you be in covenant with someone you can't or don't trust?

You must trust and be able to believe in your spouse. Trust is like a pillar supporting the relationship. If trust is broken it can be restored through repentance and forgiveness. In the Bible, Peter denied Jesus three times. Peter repented, Jesus forgave him, Peter was restored, and went on to have a great relationship with the Lord and lead many to Christ.

Everyone, deep down, wants an intimate relationship with their spouse. People want to be fully known, approved of and accepted by someone that they love and who loves them. Intimacy is more than sex. It means to have close acquaintance with someone; to know their deepest nature. If a married couple will treat each other as described in this chapter, and build trust in their relationship, intimacy will result. Don't go a minute further in your marriage without this commitment. You'll never experience God's best if you don't put this into practice.

God Hates Divorce?

At the start of this book, I compared a husband and wife to oil and water in a bottle. If you shake the bottle, the two become one; if you put the bottle away, and leave it for a while, the two will separate. Many of us are familiar with the following scripture.

> Malachi 2:16 (NKJV)
> *"For the LORD God of Israel says that He hates divorce, for it covers one's garment with violence," says the LORD of hosts. Therefore take heed to your spirit, that you do not deal treacherously."*

God hates divorce; no doubt about it. However, in the Hebrew, the word translated divorce in this scripture does not just mean divorce; it has a much broader meaning than that. The Hebrew word is "shalach," which means putting away or separation; this word describes the process of dishonoring the covenant that eventually leads to the event of divorce. Divorce is certainly included, but marital separation is also included. People who are married and sleeping in separate bedrooms are separated even though they live in the same house. They aren't keeping God happy by living in this condition; God hates this too. He wants you to honor the marriage covenant, reconcile it, and have a good relationship.

Many people stay in unhappy, bad marriages for a variety of reasons. They stay together for the kids, for economic reasons, due to social pressures, or for religious reasons because they have heard that God hates divorce. Divorce is an event, and they stay together and avoid the event. God does hate the event of divorce, but He also hates the whole process leading up to the event. That is why this word is used in this scripture. If you are honoring the covenant with your spouse—putting hesed and agape to work, there will be no putting away or divorce; it would not be possible.

I hope that you will look at where Rebekah and I started out (described in the final chapter) and see how much our lives have changed. In the beginning, we were just two separate people sharing an address. We did not have a clue about anything but ourselves. But God had a better way—a way that gave us a life together better than we could ever imagine. Our lives now are so intertwined, we truly are one. Rebekah and I are family, not just through the legal part of marriage, but because of the covenant we have before God with one another. If you would have asked us in the first year of our marriage if a marriage like this were possible, we would have probably said, "Only in storybooks." I'm glad God has a book too. In His Book are all the instructions for the best life anyone could ever dream of. I challenge you to put what He showed us to work in your marriage. Remember, any marriage, no matter how bad can be saved, and any marriage, no matter how good can be made better. No matter where you are in yours, I know this will work for you. We are living proof that this is true.

Chapter 6

Intimacy and Sex

I think any book on marriage would be incomplete without talking about intimacy. So let's look at what intimacy really means. Many people, maybe even most, think that intimacy refers mostly to the sexual relationship. This is not correct. While the sexual relationship is a part of intimacy, it is not the whole thing.

To be intimate with your spouse means to know their deepest nature. What is their deepest nature? It's how they really think and feel about things. It's where they really are spiritually. It goes far beyond what others see, feel, hear, and touch in everyday life. It involves the physical and spiritual oneness that God intended for a husband and wife.

Probably the best example of a perfectly intimate relationship is the Trinity. The Father, the Son and Holy Spirit are one God even though they are three different persons or expressions of God. In John 10:30 (NKJV) Jesus said, "I and My Father are one."

Can we compare our relationship to the Trinity? The answer is yes. In John 17: 20 – 23 Jesus tells us that He and the Father are one and that we would be one just as they are one. If we could not be one with our spouse, Jesus would not have said this.

Ephesians 5:31 (NKJV)
*"For this reason a man shall leave his father and mother and be joined
to his wife, and the two shall become one flesh."*

So how do you become intimate with your spouse? It's really not
that difficult. One thing you need to do is create an environment
where intimacy can grow. Intimacy requires three ingredients. They
are 1) a good relationship, 2) time, and 3) effort.

A Good Relationship

Intimacy can't grow where there is strife and selfishness. That
doesn't mean your relationship has to be perfect. If you're committed
to love one another with agape love, you have a good relationship. I
believe that many people truly do not know what a good
relationship looks like; or worse yet, they think a good relationship
is one in which all of the attention is on them and they get all their
needs met. Does this describe your conversations? "Well, I've talked
about me enough, why don't you tell me what you think about me?"
This isn't a good relationship.

The elements of a good relationship are described in
Romans.

Romans 12:3, 10, 13, & 18 (NKJV)
Vs. 3, *"For I say, through the grace given to me, to everyone who is
among you, not to think of himself more highly than he ought to think,
but to think soberly, as God has dealt to each one a measure of
faith."*

Vs. 10, *"Be kindly affectionate to one another with brotherly love, in
honor giving preference to one another."*

Vs. 13, *"...distributing to the needs of the saints, given to hospitality."*

Vs., 18, *"If it is possible, as much as depends on you, live peaceably with all men."*

Vs. 21, *"Do not be overcome by evil, but overcome evil with good."*

Verse 3 tells us that one of the elements of a good relationship is not to be prideful or think that you are more important than your spouse. Value your spouse; treat them the way you would want them to treat you. Verse 10 tells us that another element of a good relationship is to seek the good of your spouse and not just your own good. You should devote what you have to offer to your spouse's wellbeing. Verse 13 tells us that you should endeavor to meet the needs of your spouse; not try to manipulate them to meet your needs. Verse 18 places upon you the responsibility to make every effort to live at peace with your spouse. A lot of arguments and strife could be avoided if we would just learn to shut our mouth and not demand our own way when something happens that doesn't suit us just right. I am responsible for getting along with Rebekah even if she might not be acting just right, and vice versa. And finally, verse 21 says, it is possible to overcome evil with good. It is impossible to overcome evil with evil. Based on the law of sowing and reaping, if you sow good into your spouse, you will reap good from them.

What Romans 12 basically tells us is that we need to be other-centered in our marriage relationship. To effectively be other-centered in your marriage (to put your spouse's needs, wants, and desires first), you must know what your spouse's needs, wants and desires are. In other words, you must know them intimately.

Other centeredness and intimacy go hand in hand. I cannot be other-centered unless I know what my spouse wants, thinks, feels, needs, prefers, desires, etc. I cannot be intimate unless I am other-centered because only then will I even care what my spouse thinks, feels, needs, prefers, and desires. Many times, your spouse will only let you in on their deepest nature after they know that you are being genuine.

Often people try to be other centered based on what they believe to be true rather than on what is really true about their spouse. So they depend on what they like or on stereotypes to help them decide what they can do to serve their spouse. Let me give you a personal example of relying on a stereotype to love your spouse.

My wife Rebekah and I had been born again less than a year, and Valentine's Day was fast approaching. In previous years, before I was a Christian, I had never done very much for Rebekah by way of celebrating Valentine's Day. Holidays, including Valentine's Day, just weren't very important to me. I didn't care about them and I figured no one else should either. However, Rebekah was not like me. To her, all holidays were important, including Valentine's Day. You can certainly imagine that she got disappointed a lot at the beginning of our marriage.

For all these reasons, I wanted to make this Valentine's Day special by getting her something really nice—something that would say, "I love you", in a big way. What I decided to do was get her this really rustic looking, gnarled wicker basket with a big red, satin bow. In the basket I put a big mushy card in a red envelope, a copy of a romance novel wrapped in red paper, and a big red heart-shaped box of chocolate candy. To top it off, I was having a local florist deliver a dozen red roses to her! I just knew that this was going to be a great Valentine's gift, and that she would love it.

Now, one thing you need to know about Rebekah is that one of the things that was a huge issue in our marriage was that Rebekah did not feel like I listened to her, cared about what she thought, or valued her opinion in any way. Another thing you need to know about Rebekah was that pink roses are her favorite. It was not long after we met that I found this out; when Rebekah is given flowers she would much, much, rather receive pink roses than anything else. I, on the other hand, had always heard that red roses mean love, and that giving a dozen red roses is a really good way to tell a girl, "I LOVE YOU". I think I picked up this notion from a Hallmark greeting card commercial or something.

Wherever I had gotten it, I was absolutely certain that red roses were the right thing to give if I really wanted to express my love to Rebekah. So, even though I knew Rebekah preferred pink roses, I decided to give her red roses anyway because it was my way of expressing my love for her. That is also why I chose to wrap all the gifts in red. I wanted everything to match very nicely to show her that I loved her enough to go a little bit of extra trouble to make her feel special.

I had a slight logistical problem that contributed to my downfall, however. I wanted to give Rebekah her gifts early on Valentine's Day morning, but the florist did not deliver that early. To overcome this small obstacle, I arranged for the flowers to be delivered the evening before Valentine's Day. I figured Rebekah would enjoy getting an early gift and it would make her look forward to the next day with anticipation! Then the next morning I could take the basket of gifts out of hiding and really dazzle her with my thoughtfulness!!

So, on Valentine's Day eve, we were in the kitchen and the doorbell rang. I knew it was the florist. I got Rebekah to go answer the door. Shortly, she came back carrying the vase of red roses. She sat them on the kitchen counter and looked at them for a few seconds. Then she slowly said, "That's real nice". Then after a few more seconds she, not so slowly, said, "You know I like pink roses!" She was thinking, "He doesn't even know me and doesn't care!" She was devastated. From there on, one thing led to another and we got into a big argument over roses on the day before Valentine's Day. (We did make up later on.)

Let me explain. Rebekah was crushed because, once again, it seemed to her that I didn't care what she wanted or thought.

This had been a constant issue in our relationship. She thought I was just trying to check off the Valentine's Day box by doing something. She felt that all the work we had been doing on our marriage up to this point was not genuine. It's easy for people to get down on Rebekah when they hear this; but put yourself in her shoes. She knew that I knew she liked pink roses. Pink roses said "I love you" to her. To her, red roses looked like a half-hearted effort at best. It looked like I watched a television commercial and repeated what I saw. It looked to her like I was doing the easy thing—just to get by.

I **was** relying on a stereotype that red roses were the way to say "I love you". I "served" her based on a stereotype and not based on what I knew about her intimately. This is a self-centered approach to trying to be other centered.

You need to love your spouse God's way. Think about this. According to 1 Corinthians 13, we are fully known by God. Because He fully knows us, He can love us perfectly. He knows our needs, desires, and tendencies. Likewise, to love your spouse God's way, you also must know their needs, desires, tendencies, etc. In other words, you must know them intimately.

Time and Effort — Getting to Know Each Other Intimately

Getting to know someone intimately takes a personal investment on the part of both people. You did this when you first met. Do you remember the dating or courting process that took place in the beginning of your relationship? You no doubt spent a lot of time getting to know each other. You talked and talked; you talked on the telephone, sitting on the couch, and when you were eating. You talked all the time because you were interested in each other. You also did things like going out to eat, spending as much time together as possible, and you made a decision to get married based on what you learned.

You might think that you are spending hours with your spouse already, and this may be true. But what are you doing when you spend all this time together? If you have kids, I can tell you from experience you're not getting a lot of uninterrupted face time. It's sometimes difficult having a quality conversation while chasing a toddler. Even if your kids are older, it's hard to have intimate conversations in front of them. You might think that if you don't have kids this doesn't apply. Well, kids or no kids, if you and your spouse watch TV when you're together, how deep can the conversation go between commercials? If your countless hours together involve watching TV, or going to the movies, then all you are going to know intimately is TV and movie plots. There is usually very little conversation, especially meaningful conversation in the middle of a football game or a movie. When was the last time you learned a great deal about your spouse by the end of a bowl game? Breakfast together every morning behind a newspaper doesn't mean you've had breakfast with your spouse. Some people think they are spending hours together, but time spent together doesn't equal intimacy.

Time by itself will not lead to intimacy. In addition to time, you need to use some effort to get to know your spouse. What should this effort look like? Let's cover some things you can do to help you get to know your spouse.

Take a moment and consider times in the past when you felt the closest to your spouse. What were the characteristics of those times? Many people, when asked this question, will say they were alone together or away somewhere with their spouse. This is a good thing to think on because you want to create an atmosphere where intimacy can grow in your relationship now. These past situations can show you how to create that atmosphere. Remember, intimacy won't grow where there is strife. (If there is strife, get rid of it. If necessary, forgive and repent as we discussed in earlier chapters.)

Another important thing to understand is that men and women are different. Again, this may seem silly, but I used to think that the only difference between men and women were the obvious physical differences. I expected that women would react to situations the same way I would because I thought that women thought and felt like I did. Wrong! The differences between men and women go far beyond the physical. Not only do we differ physically, but we also think differently and we are emotionally different.

When Rebekah and I first got married I used to try to base all of my decisions on "logical reasoning." A lot of men do this. Rebekah would consider logic, but she would bring how she felt emotionally into the process too. That used to frustrate me to no end and I didn't understand it. Rebekah would try to remind me that just because I thought something did not make it so.

One of the biggest revelations you can get in life is this—not everyone is like you, and that doesn't mean you are right and they are wrong; this includes your spouse. Think about it and read it again. This alone could change your life. Your spouse probably has many different needs, wants, desires, tastes, and preferences than you do. This is normal. It doesn't mean they are wrong. It doesn't mean you are wrong, either. Different doesn't equal wrong. It equals different.

So, just remember, and expect, that men and women are different. They are different emotionally, physically, and genetically. This does not mean that one is better than the other. Galatians 3:28 says that we are all one in Jesus Christ - there is no male or female in Him. That means in His eyes we are equal. So the husband is not better than the wife, and vice versa.

So what are some other ways we can be other centered toward each other? You need to seek to meet your spouse's needs above your own. In other words, you need to minister to your spouse and not to yourself. The opposite of ministry is manipulation. A lot of people try to get their spouse to meet their needs by manipulating them. Did you ever have an acquaintance or know someone who would be really friendly to you when they wanted something from you? That is manipulation.

When you know that someone is manipulating you (just plain old using you), you don't want to be around them, much less be close or intimate with them. In fact, you'll probably try to avoid them. On the other hand, once you know that someone genuinely has your best interests at heart and cares about you, you won't mind opening up to them. This is what we need to do in our marriage relationship.

We should spend time alone together. Have you ever heard of the "empty nest" syndrome? It's when a married couple's kids have grown up and left the home - the nest is empty. This couple suddenly doesn't know what to do with their time. Often, they haven't taken care to maintain their marriage relationship through the years, and when the kids are gone, they are left with someone they really don't know anymore. They have grown apart and have no common interest anymore because they let their marriage fall on the priority list.

It is very natural to be saddened by children leaving "the nest." But it should also be a wonderful time for a married couple. It can be even better than when the kids were home. Usually, your financial situation is better than when you first married, so you could be free to do things you couldn't do when you had children. Plus, you don't have a tight schedule with school or sports activities, so you're free to do other things. You can travel, go out more, and get involved in your own activities together.

It's important to maintain your relationship with your spouse. It's amazing, but people often ask, "How do I do that?" Well, how did you get to know them in the first place? You spent time with them. And it wasn't just time spent watching TV or reading the paper either. You went to dinner together. You went for walks together. You talked about your dreams, hopes, and aspirations. What is your spouse's dream? What is their favorite color? If they could take a vacation anywhere in the world, where would they go? We ought to know these things. Don't feel bad if you don't—go find out!! One more thing, it can be difficult to get to know your spouse intimately when you are at home, or with other people. These things tend to be distractions that remove your focus from your spouse. You should date your spouse at least once a month if not more often. If you go to a movie, do something else too. In the movie, you are getting to know the movie and not your spouse. Go out to eat first. Talk about the movie afterwards and what you think or feel about it. Make sure you interact with each other; otherwise you are missing the whole point.

Communication

Now let's discuss communication. Communication is a very important key to intimacy. In fact, some people say that communication is the biggest problem in marriage. I don't agree with this. After all, you can communicate and communicate and communicate and still wind up in an argument. Self-centeredness is the problem.

But communication is certainly a major symptom that must be addressed. Information communicated can be used against your spouse to manipulate them. So, more communication isn't necessarily the answer. What you do with the information that is communicated is the key.

Proverbs 13:17 (TLB)
"Reliable communication permits progress."

Without a doubt, you want to have forward progress in

your marriage relationship. Good communication is essential to that. Communication should be viewed as a tool to learn more about your spouse so that you can serve their needs better. It isn't unusual for two people to be saying the same thing, but due to faulty communications they don't even know it. This happens to Rebekah and me occasionally now, but it used to happen to us a lot. I would say something and what Rebekah would hear wasn't what I meant. Communication can be difficult. Sometimes you know exactly what you are trying to say and your spouse has no idea. Consider these real examples from insurance claims:

- "I had been driving for forty years when I fell asleep at the wheel and had an accident."
- "I cannot get sick pay. I have six children. Can you tell me why?"
- "I am glad to report that my husband who was reported missing is dead."
- "The guy was all over the road. I had to swerve several times before I hit him."
- "I pulled away from the side of the road, glanced at my mother-in-law and headed over the embankment."

And how about these supposedly true excerpts from church bulletins?

- Don't let worry kill you - let the church help.
- Thursday night - Potluck supper. Prayer and medication to follow.
- Remember in prayer the many who are sick of our church and community.
- For those of you who have children and didn't know it, we have a nursery downstairs.
- The rosebud on the alter this morning is to announce the

birth of David Alan Belzer, the sin of Rev. and Mrs. Julius
Belzer.

- The 'Over 60s Choir' will be disbanded for the summer
  with the thanks of the entire church.

- Ladies, don't forget the rummage sale next weekend. It is
  a good chance to get rid of all those things not worth
  keeping around the house. Bring your husbands.

- The sermon this morning: Jesus Walks on the Water. The
  sermon tonight: Searching for Jesus.

- Our parishioner, Barbara C. remains in the hospital and
  needs blood donors for more transfusions. She is also
  having trouble sleeping and requests tapes of the Pastor's
  sermons.

- The ladies of the church have cast off clothing of every
  kind. They can be seen in the church basement Saturday.

- At the evening service tonight, the sermon topic will
  be "What is Hell?" Come early and listen to our choir
  practice.

- The peace-making meeting scheduled for today has been
  canceled due to a conflict.

As you can see from these examples, communication can come out
wrong even if you know exactly what you are trying to say. You need to
make sure your spouse knows what you are trying to say, and also make
sure you understand what your spouse is trying to say. Just because
you understand does not mean that they understand you.
Remember, if you are trying to communicate something, and the
person your relaying the message to doesn't understand what you've
said, it's not their fault. It is your responsibility as the communicator to
get the other person to hear and understand. Most of the time we
think it's the listener's job. Sometimes we'll even become angry or
short because they didn't understand. If you are the one
communicating, you are responsible.

We used to have pink flannel sheets that Rebekah liked to use on our bed in winter. I remember one time we had just gone to bed and Rebekah rolled over and pulled some of the sheet with her. I jokingly said, "You're hogging the pink sheet." She said, "What did you say?" I told her again and then asked, "What did you think I said?" She said, "I thought you called me a hog in the pig sheet!" You know, a miscommunication like that could result in a big argument. Thank goodness she thought it was funny.

Another important aspect of communication is the need to be transparent. This can be difficult because transparency involves risk due to the fear of rejection. After all, if you open up your inner most self and share something from the heart, your spouse could possibly ridicule or reject you. It takes time to develop a level of trust to be transparent. They key to transparency is using what is communicated to minister to your spouse rather than manipulate them. Then trust will grow, fear of rejection will leave, and greater transparency will be the result. This issue is addressed in the scripture below.

1 John 4:18 (NKJV)
"There is no fear in love; but perfect love casts out fear, because fear involves torment. But he who fears has not been made perfect in love."

This proves from the Word that as you walk in love and minister to your spouse, fear will disappear. In an atmosphere of love, there is no fear of rejection and thus you feel free to be transparent.

When Rebekah and I first got married, she was very insecure, and I didn't give her any reason to think that I was committed to her. I was constantly doing my own thing. When we got married, we went to a justice of the peace. It wasn't what Rebekah wanted, but I figured it was good enough. She had bought a wedding dress and wanted a wedding, but I figured that was too much trouble and would cost too much money. Rather than me taking a day (or even a morning) off of work to get married, we went on a Saturday morning. After the Saturday morning vows, Rebekah wanted to go out for breakfast to celebrate. I was being contrary and didn't want to go; I didn't want her to get what she wanted. I didn't want to start out like that. I wanted to be in charge, so I said, "Let's just go home." (We had lived together for about six months prior to getting married).

So we started home, and I thought, "She's going to think I want to go straight home to consummate the marriage." This was a normal thing to do after people get married, but to me at the time, I thought, "She's not going to control me." I know that sounds crazy, but I wanted to control this relationship. She wasn't trying to control me; she just wanted me to love her. Instead, I used what I thought I knew to keep her at a distance and manipulate the situation. This event produced a lot of hurt and insecurity in our relationship. To get to transparency in communication requires using what is communicated to minister. Using it to manipulate results in the building of walls, which is the opposite of transparency, and that can never lead to intimacy.

So how do you communicate? I am glad you asked. The Bible provides us with an excellent formula to use for effective communication. It is found in James.

James 1:19 (NKJV)
"So then, my beloved brethren, let every man be swift to hear, slow to speak, slow to wrath."

Did you get that? Effective communication requires three things from us. First it requires that we listen. Be sure you understand what your spouse is trying to communicate to you. Understanding is the most important thing. Don't try to keep track of who is winning or losing. All too often we make an assumption based on the first few words they say, and we only pretend to listen to the rest. Or we start to judge what we think they are saying. We need to listen completely. Second, we need to be slow to speak. Many times we might seem to be listening, but what we are doing is preparing our response. Once we have a response ready, we might even cut our spouse off before they are finished and start talking ourselves. This is not being slow to speak. Finally, we need to be slow to wrath. Just don't get angry. In 1 Corinthians 15:31 the apostle Paul said, "...I die daily....". He isn't referring to a literal, physical death. He is talking about putting his wants, needs and desires second and ministering to others day in and day out. When our spouse communicates something we don't like, our flesh rises up and wants to get mad. We have to not let our wants, feelings, desires, and emotions rule us; this is called dying to the flesh. It is impossible for a dead man to get angry. Anger on the part of one person will almost always result in anger on the part of the other. If the Apostle Paul had to die daily, then I probably need to die about every five minutes—maybe even more often than that. In short, listen, be quiet, and don't get mad.

Here are a few other tips for communication. Pray for God's wisdom. He may show you that you are in the wrong. If you need to talk, plan a time that is good for your spouse. When Rebekah and I first got married, she liked to save serious conversations for bedtime. There were a couple of times that I fell asleep on her while she was telling me something important. You can bet that did not go over well with her! Make sure you set aside time for your spouse every day or bedtime might be the only time they can get your attention. Ephesians 4:15 says we should speak the truth in love. God's Word, not your opinion, is the truth, and even when your conversation is Word based, you should speak in love. Love needs to be your motivation. Ask yourself what is best for your relationship, not what is best for you.

Finally, and without this the communication process won't accomplish anything, act on what is communicated. Use what is communicated to minister to your spouse. Use it to love them and serve them and meet their needs. Take what you learn and use it to make their life better.

The Birds and the Bees

The physical or sexual relationship is more than a biological function. A spiritual union takes place also (See 1 Corinthians 6:16) in which two become one. It is a renewal of the marriage covenant. This is further explained in Ephesians.

Ephesians 5:31 and 32 (NKJV)
"For this reason a man shall leave his father and mother and be joined to his wife, and the two shall become one flesh. This is a great mystery, but I speak concerning Christ and the church."

The sexual relationship is an important part of marriage. It needs to be talked about in the context of Christianity and the Bible. The scriptures in many places are pretty straightforward when it comes to this subject. The Bible used to be read aloud in the temple, so it is OK to talk about sex. In fact it should be taught in our churches. Many Christian couples don't know what is right and wrong in this area because it isn't taught that often in church.

Still, some people get nervous when you talk about sex, but God created it as a gift in marriage. Since God created sex, Christians should know what God thinks about it. We need to learn about sex in a way that glorifies God, strengthens our marriage, and brings pleasure to both covenant partners. The sexual relationship can, and should, do all of that. Sex is a holy act in marriage. The world looks at sex differently than God. God's view on sex is found in 1 Corinthians.

1 Corinthians 7:1-4 (MSG)

"...Is it a good thing to have sexual relations? Certainly—but only within a certain context. It's good for a man to have a wife, and for a woman to have a husband. Sexual drives are strong, but marriage is strong enough to contain them and provide for a balanced and fulfilling sexual life in a world of sexual disorder. The marriage bed must be a place of mutuality—the husband seeking to satisfy his wife, the wife seeking to satisfy her husband. Marriage is not a place to 'stand up for your rights'. Marriage is a decision to serve the other, whether in bed or out. "

Notice that the marriage bed is a place to serve and not be served. Notice also that sex is reserved for marriage. Do you think of sex as a Holy, God ordained act reserved for people who are married? Most people think of everything but that. Sex today is viewed as a one person thing and a way to gratify the flesh. It has been perverted to a completely self-centered act, fueled by the insecurities of the people involved. Many men want to have sex to puff up their egos so they can think of themselves as real men, studs, etc. This is a misconception. Sex proves nothing about being a man. Many women have sex because they are looking for love and acceptance. They mistakenly think that having sex will make a man love them. In both cases it is all about self and many times it is taking place outside of marriage.

Sex is also widely used as an advertising tool. A lot of the models in advertising are standing by a product with lustful expressions on their face and a posture that makes it look sexy. The ad seems to say, "I or someone like me and sex will come as a result of you buying this product." Or it is saying, "You will be much sexier" if you have whatever the ad is selling. Just in case you don't know, this is completely untrue.

The world tells us that sex is about using someone to get your desires fulfilled. It seems to have nothing to do with a holy act and everything to do with a self-centered desire. Sex in marriage, on the other hand, is an intimate act that renews the covenant between the married couple. Sex in the world is not about giving; it's about taking. It has little to do with a couple bound by covenant and a lot to do with a conquering mentality that is out for self-satisfaction.

Sex between a married couple is the single most intimate act shared between them. Hebrews speaks about the marital sexual relationship.

> Hebrews 13:4 (AMP)
> *"Let marriage be held in honor (esteemed worthy, precious, of great price, and especially dear) in all things. And thus let the marriage bed be undefiled (kept undishonored); for God will judge and punish the unchaste [all guilty of sexual vice] and adulterous."*

You may be thinking this scripture is only talking about being physically faithful to your spouse. There is more to this scripture than that. When it says, *"let the marriage bed be undefiled (kept undishonored)"*, it is talking about contaminating the marriage bed. How else could you contaminate it other than cheating? One way is by mixing it or mingling it with other things. Do you casually talk about your sex life with other people? If you do, you are mixing your sex life with others. You are bringing someone else into this intimate relationship that should only be shared by you and your spouse. It contaminates the marriage bed.

Think about it—if you talk about your sex life with other people, you could be painting pictures of you and your spouse in their minds; certainly you don't want that. The sexual relationship should be between the husband and wife only. I'm not talking about a situation where there may be a need to get counseling regarding the sexual relationship. If you need counsel in this area, seek the assistance of a professional. We are talking about gossiping, boasting or complaining about your sex life with your friends.

Sex between a married couple should get better and better as the years go by just like the marriage relationship should get better and better. Sex in the first year of marriage should be great, but sex in the tenth or twentieth years and beyond should be even better. Some people think the longer they are married, they'll get tired of each other and sex will get boring. But this is not true.

How can it get better and better? If you learn to satisfy each other you can better serve each other's needs in bed. Men and women are different. Men can typically achieve sexual arousal more quickly than women. This difference alone makes for some challenges in the sexual relationship. There needs to be communication between the husband and wife about their sexual needs. Just because things seem fine for one doesn't mean things are fine for the other. This is especially true when people first get married. At the beginning of a marriage we have certain assumptions and a lot of uncertainty about how the sexual relationship should work. Frankly, most people approach it self-centeredly and are chiefly concerned about whether it is good for them. Lack of communication and no effort to improve will result in an unsatisfying sex life for the husband and the wife. You've seen the stereotypical situations where the husband is constantly pursuing more sex and the wife is constantly thinking of ways to avoid it.

In marriage, it is far more common for the wife to have a less satisfying sex life than the husband. Why is that? It is simply because the two do not take the time to learn how to please each other. It is the wife's job to teach her husband how to satisfy her, and it is the husband's job to learn how to please his wife. Deuteronomy references just how important it is to learn to please your spouse.

Deuteronomy 24:5 (NKJV)
"When a man has taken a new wife, he shall not go out to war or be charged with any business; he shall be free at home one year, and bring happiness to his wife whom he has taken."

This clearly shows that a man needs to give attention to pleasing his wife and not just himself. Men and women aren't "wired" the same. Males and females typically are sexually aroused in different ways. We should teach each other what our individual needs are. Men sometimes think that women are the same in the sexual arena as they are. If the wife doesn't teach her husband about her needs, and if the husband does not give attention to learning her needs, sex will become unfulfilling to the wife and frustrating to the husband. A lot of women become uninterested in it all together because of this very thing.

Sex is a really important part of marriage. I think few people realize how important a healthy sexual relationship is to the life of a marriage. When a husband and wife have sexual relations, they are remembering the covenant between them and they are honoring and renewing it. Remember, sex is reserved for the marriage covenant alone.

In fact, the sexual relationship between a husband and wife has many parallels with the taking of communion. Think about it. In the sexual relationship, the two become one flesh. In communion, we eat bread which symbolizes the body of Christ. By eating it we symbolize that we are one with Him. Just as sex honors and recalls the marriage covenant, so communion honors and recalls our covenant with God. 1 Corinthians 11:27 – 30, discusses how important is to take communion in a worthy manner; verse 30 specifically says that taking communion in an unworthy manner is why many Christians are weak, sick, or die early. This is the only place I know of in the New Testament that says how we as Christians can bring weakness, sickness, and death upon ourselves. Now think of this in the context of marriage. If we approach the sexual relationship with a self-serving motive, I believe we will weaken, sicken, and possibly kill the marriage relationship—and we did it to ourselves.

So, serve each other in the marriage bed. Have some conversations about it. Ask questions and be open. It may be uncomfortable at first, but keep in mind you're in covenant with this person, and your sex life is a gift that God has given to you both.

Suppose you received a car as a gift. You have to learn a lot of things in the beginning such as where the lights are, where the wipers are, how to operate the radio, etc. But once you learn what makes the car work, it becomes less "mechanical" and more natural. The more natural it becomes, the more enjoyable it is. The same is true with the physical relationship. The more you know, the more enjoyable it can be.

It is common for marriage partners to have different sex drives. One may want it every day and the other may think once a week is plenty. What do you do in these situations? There are different options, but it's more important to have a plan in place than to "play it by ear." One option might be to decide that sex is always a good idea. Maybe another option could be to occasionally say "not tonight" as long as it is used sparingly. Whatever you decide between yourselves, decide something. If you don't have some plan in place, a lot of hurt and rejection can take place which can create all sorts of problems within the marriage. Sometimes what is not communicated can cause people to make assumptions, and this can be a lot worse than the reality of the situation. Again, you need to approach the sexual relationship in a right manner to help ensure a strong marriage.

While we're here on this subject of sex drives, let's discuss a problem some people have in this area. Some people use masturbation as the answer when one spouse's sex drive is greater than the other's. If their spouse isn't in the mood, they figure they can take care of themselves. Maybe the unwilling spouse even thinks it is a good idea if you just go somewhere and masturbate as long as you leave them alone and as long as you are thinking about them while doing it. Masturbation has no place in the marriage. Frankly it has no place in life whatsoever. It can do great harm to a marriage. Masturbation serves self. It is lust based. Anything that purely serves self can become an addiction. Think about it, masturbation involves fantasizing. You don't masturbate without fantasizing about someone else. Your spouse can't compete with a fantasy, even if you are fantasizing about them. In a fantasy, you can manipulate them to do whatever you want. You know your sexual desires better than anyone and in a fantasy you can have them all fulfilled. You can totally serve yourself without regard for them. A fantasy also has no flaws, and no one is perfect. No one can compete with perfection. So even if you are only thinking of your spouse, your spouse will never be able to compete with a fantasy. Self-centeredness in this area can lead you down a road where you never thought you would go.

Let's examine this subject in light of scripture.

Matthew 5:28 (NKJV)
"But I say to you that whoever looks at a woman to lust for her has already committed adultery with her in his heart."

Are those fantasies OK? No. Not only is it not OK, but your spouse can start to prefer masturbation and fantasy over the real deal. It could come to the point that they have to fantasize in order to have sex with you. This can cause real problems in the sexual relationship.

1 Corinthians 6:18 (AMP)
"Shun immorality and all sexual looseness [flee from impurity in thought, word, or deed]. Any other sin which a man commits is one outside the body, but he who commits sexual immorality sins against his own body."

Most people don't understand what this scripture means when it says sexual sin is a sin against your own body. You are one with your spouse—Ephesians 5:29 even says we should love our wives as our own body. Adam called Eve, "bone of my bones and flesh of my flesh." Therefore, your sexual sin is a sin against you and your spouse's body.

Many people have never thought of it this way, but masturbation is sex outside of marriage – that is a sin. Masturbation is a sin and it is harmful to marriage. It is addictive, and any addiction can hold you captive. Don't let it ruin your marriage. I have heard it said before that sin will take you farther than you want to go and cost you more than you want to pay. It just isn't worth it.

I have heard people say it is better to masturbate than to burn with lust. The Bible disagrees with that. We saw above where the Bible says in 1 Corinthians 7 that marriage is strong enough to contain sexual desires. It also has the following to say regarding lust.

1 Corinthians 7:9 (NLT)
"But if they can't control themselves, they should go ahead and marry. It's better to marry than to burn with lust."

Did God say it is better to masturbate than burn with lust? No! He—the Creator of both marriage and sex—says to get married to take care of that issue. Sex is meant for marriage. Period. If anyone says masturbation is OK—that it is better than adultery or thinking lustful thoughts, they are basically telling you it is OK to choose what they consider to be the lesser sin. However, we are the ones that grade sins. As far as God is concerned, sin is sin, and all sin separates you from God.

Finally, masturbation does not produce good fruit. The Bible teaches us to judge things by its fruit (Matthew 7:16). Some actions produce good fruit and some bad fruit. Masturbation, taken to its end, will not produce good fruit. The bad fruit it can produce include addiction, unfaithfulness in your marriage, an unbalanced sex life, and a weak marriage.

Let's move on and take a look at how God wants the sexual

relationship to work. 1 Corinthians provides us with some great insights.

1 Corinthians 7:3-5 (CEV)
Vs. 3: *"The husband should not deprive his wife of sexual intimacy, which is her right as a married woman, nor should the wife deprive her husband."*

Vs. 4: *"The wife gives authority over her body to her husband, and the husband also gives authority over his body to his wife."*

Vs. 5: *"So do not deprive each other of sexual relations. The only exception to this rule would be the agreement of both husband and wife to refrain from sexual intimacy for a limited time, so they can give themselves more completely to prayer. Afterward they should come together again so that Satan won't be able to tempt them because of their lack of self-control."*

These scriptures give us three principles that can be used as a guide for our sex lives. Verse three says that both people have needs. Sex is for both the husband and the wife and should be enjoyed by both. Verse four says that when we get married our bodies do not belong to us anymore. As noted earlier, you may have different desires as far as the sex drive is concerned, so have a plan in place. If necessary change your thinking to reflect that sex is always a good idea. Verse five says not to deprive each other. Get into the habit of having sex.

As I said before, women and men think differently when it comes to sex. Most women think in terms of romance and then sex follows that. For most women it is an emotional experience as well as a physical one. For a woman, sex can start in the morning in the form of romance; it may even start days in advance. Most wives need romance as a prelude to sex. They need emotional arousal before they get aroused physically. On the other hand, most men are stimulated by sight. They can see their wife walk by, and they are ready right now! So, men, if you want sex more often, increase the romance and get to know her needs in the emotional and sexual arena. If you apply what you learn, if you serve her in this area as scripture instructs, your sex life will greatly improve. If you want her to adopt the attitude that sex is always a good idea, be willing to meet her needs in the romantic and emotional area.

One of the goals of sex is to reach climax or orgasm—the moment of most intense pleasure in sexual intercourse. The word climax comes from the Greek word "kl max" which literally means "ladder." How do you reach the highest point on a ladder? You climb up one rung at a time. Men and women "climb the climax ladder" at different speeds. Usually, the man reaches the peak more quickly than the woman does. However, orgasm for both men and women is more intense when foreplay comes first. That's right; even a man gets maximum sexual release with about 30 minutes of arousal beforehand. What are we saying? Don't rush sex! Especially you husbands. The key to you having a great sex life is for you to make sure it is great for your wife.

One thing people often ask us is what they can and can't do as far as sex is concerned. We tell them that if your spouse feels convicted about not doing a certain thing, don't pressure them even if you feel it's o.k. If you pressure them, you are making them to go against their conscience, and it will make them feel condemned. You don't want any condemnation concerning your physical relationship.

We have also been asked about "role playing". For those that do not know, this is when people pretend to be someone other than who they are, i.e., a stewardess, a doctor, or even wearing a wig. Our thoughts on this...we don't think it is wise. It may bring pleasure for the moment, but it opens the door to the devil to bring thoughts to your spouse. Thoughts like, "I wonder if my spouse desires to be with someone with a different hair color or with a different profession. This is only the beginning of doubt and lies the devil will bring into your marriage. It can cause great insecurity in your relationship which can cause terrible problems. Be who you are. Don't ever make your spouse feel they need to be something or someone they are not.

Conclusion

Intimacy is important. You need to know your spouse—truly know them. Until you do, you cannot serve them the way that God desires. I believe that you are God's chosen minister to your spouse. Think about it. You have a covenant relationship with your spouse, and you don't have a relationship like that with any other human being, not even your kids. Out of three billion plus men on this earth, I am the one anointed by God to be Rebekah's husband. The same is true for her. You are the anointed one for your spouse. You are God's chosen minister to them. If your spouse is going to experience God's love on this earth, God is going to use you as the primary means of expressing that love to them. In order to love them God's way, you are going to have to know them intimately.

Chapter 7

A LOOK AT ROLES

We are nearing the end of this book. We have chosen to wait until now to cover a subject that many people discuss first when talking about marriage relationships -the roles of the husband and wife. Why? Because we truly believe that if you apply the things discussed in the previous chapters, the roles of the husband and wife will largely work themselves out. Many people have a distorted understanding of the roles of a husband and wife. We hope to bring some clarity in this chapter.

The Husband's Role—A Hard Look at the Head

The Bible says that the husband is the head of the wife. The scriptures that back this up are found below.

1 Corinthians 11:3 (AMP)
"But I want you to know and realize that Christ is the Head of every man, the head of a woman is her husband, and the Head of Christ is God."

Ephesians 5:23 (NKJV)

"For the husband is head of the wife, as also Christ is head of the church; and He is the Savior of the body."

This isn't popular information with many people, but it is true nonetheless. Please understand that God is not trying to make women miserable by making the husband the head; on the contrary, Jesus said He came to give abundant life. The marriage relationship is intended to contribute to the abundant life He offers. The reason this concept is so disagreeable to many is because true headship is so often misunderstood by men and women. If you understand what headship really is, and what the responsibilities of the role are, you will have a lot less trouble accepting it.

First off, let's define headship. It is an office of authority <u>and</u> responsibility. Many people only look at the first part of that definition—authority. Yes, the head does have authority, but he also has responsibility. Oftentimes the authority is over emphasized and the responsibilities are overlooked. We will look at the responsibilities first. The reason for this is because if you understand the responsibilities that the husband has, you will better see that he needs the authority to fulfill them.

What are the responsibilities of the head? As always, we will look to the Bible to find out. As the scriptures above show, the Bible says the husband is to be the head of the wife as Christ is the head of the Church. In other words, Jesus is the husband's example for headship. Therefore, husbands can learn how to function in their role by studying how Jesus functions as the head of the Church. It is the responsibility of Christian husbands to imitate Jesus' example of headship. Anything else will not provide a perfect example of headship.

In studying Jesus' example of headship, I have found a number of characteristics that seem to be missing in many marriages. Again, many husbands think being the head means, "I'm in charge here—I'm the boss." This is only a fraction of the truth and it alone will not contribute to success in marriage. Let's look at some important aspects of Jesus' example of headship that should be copied by the husband.

The Number One Responsibility of the Head

The number one responsibility of the head is probably also the most overlooked responsibility.

1 John 3:8b (NKJV)

"For this purpose the Son of God was manifested, that He might destroy the works of the devil."

Jesus came to destroy the works of the devil. That begs a question. What are the works of the devil? I suppose we could make a list that would easily be beyond the scope of this book. But we just need to look at the first works of the devil, and that was to separate man from God and then separate husband from wife. This happened in the Garden of Eden. When man ate the fruit it resulted in the separation of man from God. We see separation of husband and wife, when Adam pointed the finger and blamed Eve for what had happened. Causing division in relationships was the first and primary work of the devil. Jesus, the head, came to destroy the devil's works.

Think about what Jesus did on Earth. He reconciled the relationship between man and God. The husband, as the head of the wife, is to imitate this in the marriage relationship. The husband has the primary responsibility for keeping the marriage relationship reconciled.

This has gotten turned upside down to the point that, in much of society, the wife takes care of relationships and the husband takes care of himself. That is not God's plan, it is not what Jesus did as the head, and it will not result in the best for your marriage. This is a critical part of the husband's role. It is something that husbands are anointed to do, and something they should not shirk.

Other Responsibilities of Headship

In addition to having the primary responsibility for keeping the marriage reconciled, the husband has several other responsibilities. These are all things that Jesus did in fulfilling His role as the head.

The head should walk in love. Jesus walked in love at all times. Love was inseparable from Jesus' day-to-day life; it defined who He was. You as husband should do the same. Christ's love is unconditional (as seen in Romans 8:38 and 39 which we discussed in Chapter 4). Ephesians 5:25 says the husband is to love the wife in this same unconditional way. Many husbands have a "John Wayne" mentality toward love, emotions, and intimacy. Don't get me wrong. I like a good John Wayne movie as much as anyone does, but you shouldn't model your personality after his. It seems to me that in a lot of his movies he was either separated from his wife or there was a woman who loved him but couldn't stand to be around him. Does this sound like a recipe for a good relationship to you? I don't think so! A husband needs to learn how his wife receives love and make sure to love her in that way. Act like she is the most important relationship in your life, because next to God, she is. Spend time listening to her, talking to her, and learning to love her.

The head should be other centered. The first chapter of this book talks about the problem of self-centeredness and all of the problems it causes. The head simply can't be selfish. Jesus wasn't selfish. He put others first. The husband should do the same.

The head should be faithful. Jesus was faithful. He was even faithful when others were not. Peter denied Jesus three times, but after Jesus was resurrected, He made a point to restore Peter. That's faithfulness. Think of this; when Adam fell in the Garden of Eden, God could have tossed mankind and started over. He had the right to do it. Man had broken relationship with Him by sinning.

Instead, so great was his commitment and faithfulness to man, that He sent Jesus, His only son. Jesus knew that He would suffer horrendously to fulfill God's plan of redemption. Yet Hebrews 12:2 says that for the joy set before Him, He endured the pain of the cross. That is faithfulness! Christ sets a clear example that the head is to be uncompromisingly faithful. This is reinforced in Malachi.

Malachi 2:14 & 15 (CEV)

"And why isn't God pleased? It's because he knows that each of you men has been unfaithful to the wife you married when you were young. You promised that she would be your partner, but now you have broken that promise. Didn't God create you to become like one person with your wife? And why did he do this? It was so you would have children, and then lead them to become God's people. Don't ever be unfaithful to your wife."

Husbands must be faithful to their wives. Faithfulness goes beyond just the sexual relationship. How so? Well, do you ever enjoy a laugh at your spouse's expense? Do you ever put her down to other people when she isn't around (or when she is around)? Those are ways of breaking faith. Be faithful. Can she depend on you to do what you say? Are you there to help when she needs you?

The head should honor the wife. If the President of the United States were to show up on your doorstep you would no doubt be honored at his visit and you would treat him with honor. Why? Because, in our estimation, the President is a very important person; he should be treated with honor. The same holds true and even more so if Jesus showed up on your doorstep. You would honor Him. Why? It's because he is the Son of God. He deserves to be treated with honor.

Now think about this. The Bible says that Christians are joint heirs with Christ; that we are children of God (John 1:12) just as Jesus is God's child. We treat people we think are important with honor. Should we also treat people that God thinks are important with honor? Your spouse is a child of God. In God's estimation, she is very important. So important in fact that He is willing to die for her. She can't get much more important than that! Your spouse should be treated with honor by you. In fact, when you dishonor your spouse, you dishonor God.

In 1 Peter 3:7 it specifically says that husbands are to honor their wife. What does it mean to honor someone? That's easy. Just treat them the way we would want to be treated. Treat them the way you would treat someone you deem highly important. Some hints are to be considerate, listen to what they say, respect them and their opinions, be nice to them, talk to them, tell them you love them, act like you love them, give them credit where it is due, esteem them, and regard them highly.

The head should provide for the family. The Bible tells us that God meets all of our needs by His riches in glory by Christ Jesus (Philippians 4:19). Jesus certainly provided for the people in His life in a variety of ways. He fed them. He protected them; remember when He calmed the storm? He soothed their emotional hurts. When Lazarus' sister was emotionally distraught at Lazarus' death, Jesus comforted her (John 11:17 – 33). He continues to provide for us in many ways today. Jesus provided for them spiritually; He died so that we could have life. His life showed us how to live. So we see that Jesus provided for them physically, emotionally, and spiritually.

Likewise, the Bible says in 1Timothy 5:8 that the man is to provide for the family. Here again, Jesus is our example. The husband is responsible for providing for the family. This includes providing for them financially, but as shown by Jesus, it goes beyond that.

The Husband is primarily responsible for the physical, emotional, and spiritual provision of His family. There should be no excuses and no passing the buck to the wife. She can help, but she shouldn't have the responsibility. The husband has the responsibility; He is called by God to do it. When God calls you to do something, He equips you and anoints you to do it. We are not saying that the wife cannot work, but do not put this responsibility solely on her. God may lead her to work while the husband is going to school or some other circumstance. But the responsibility of provision should not be pushed off to her just because she is working. You as the head should believe God for provision. The wife was not meant to shoulder this responsibility. God told the head to provide. Therefore, the husband is the one equipped and anointed to do the providing. A family will not function in the fullness of what God has if the husband does not fulfill this role.

Some men expect their wives to be the spiritual one. They want their wife to hear from God. In this area, they will defer to their wife for direction. Having a wife that can hear from God is a blessing. But, the husband should not rely on that. He needs to hear from God for himself and for direction for the family. If he doesn't, then he is not the spiritual head of the home. Build yourself up in prayer, read the Word, and learn to be led by the Spirit. This is a critical part of headship.

The head should be humble. Many people think that humility is an undesirable characteristic in a man. That's because they don't understand what humble means. They think it is wimpy. This is totally incorrect. Humble simply means to be completely under the authority of another. Just as Jesus was totally submitted to God, we are to be totally submitted to Jesus.

Philippians 2:8 (NKJV)

"And being found in appearance as a man, He humbled Himself and became obedient to the point of death, even the death of the cross."

It is by humbling yourself and doing things God's way that success comes to you in life. God's way may not be your way, but God is smarter than you are. Humility leads to promotion. James bears this out.

James 4:10 (NKJV)

"Humble yourselves in the sight of the Lord, and He will lift you up."

To the degree that you aren't humble, you are in rebellion against God; you can't expect blessings if that describes you! A wimp could not have done the things Jesus did. He was humble—submitted to God—and He totally succeeded in the mission God had for Him. This is a key to your success also - be submitted.

The head should be meek. Meekness is also misunderstood and therefore looked poorly on. In most people's minds, meek means week. However, being meek means to show patience and humility. You could say that meekness means to lead a lifestyle of humility. That's a good thing. Jesus certainly lived a lifestyle of humility. Numbers 12:3 tells us that Moses was the meekest man alive. Think about the power that Moses had working in his life. Think of the challenges he faced in dealing with Pharaoh and leading millions of Israelites out of Egypt, through the wilderness, and up to the Promised Land. Certainly Moses was not week! He had this power in his life because he was meek, leading a life of being humble to God. Don't believe the lie that meekness equals weakness. The truth is that meek and weak have opposite meanings. To be meek is to possess power in your life.

The Head's Authority

The authority of the head largely depends on the fulfillment of the primary responsibility of the head, keeping the relationship reconciled. The husband does have authority, but people often don't know what that means. Brace yourself! The husband's authority comes from his responsibility to sacrifice himself and put his family first. Think of this; only after His crucifixion did Jesus say all authority had been given to Him (refer to Matthew 28:18 and Philippians 2:9). Likewise, only after the husband lays down his own life does he truly function as the head. I'm not talking about physical death; I'm talking about putting your wife and family first.

Here is an example of the head in action. Suppose a husband and wife get into an argument and both get upset and offended with each other. Suppose also that the wife is the one in the wrong and the husband was right about whatever started the argument. Who has the greater responsibility to reconcile the relationship? Our natural mind and our emotions tell us that the person who is in the wrong has the greater responsibility. In this case that would mean the wife should apologize to the husband. That seems logical, and she should. But as the head, the husband is primarily responsible for going to the wife and getting the relationship reconciled even though the wife is the one in the wrong.

Why should this be? Here again, Jesus is our example. Consider man's relationship with God before Jesus came. It was man that was in the wrong. It was man that had sinned against God. God didn't do anything wrong. Yet it was God who came to Earth in the form of a man to reconcile the relationship between God and mankind.

So you see, this is a scriptural thing to do. Romans tells us so.

Romans 5:8 (KJV)

"While we were yet sinners, Christ died for us."

The number one job that Jesus, the Head, had when He came to
Earth was to reconcile man to God, even though He had done nothing
wrong. That is an example for you as a husband. Since Jesus paid the
price and came to make things right even when we were in the wrong,
you as a husband should do the same. The head has the primary
responsibility to keep the relationship reconciled.

Maybe you are thinking, "That makes no sense if she is the one
that is wrong." But think about it. How often is anyone ever really 100%
in the wrong? Probably never. You are at least partially at fault too. I
once heard a preacher with a national ministry say that there are only
two times when you have to say you are sorry. One is when you are in
the wrong and the other is when you aren't.

There is something I always tell people that we counsel with in
marriage. It's this. *"Being right is highly overrated. The relationship is
more important than who's right and who's wrong."* Romans 5:8,
which is quoted above, shows that God also considers the
relationship to be more important than who is right and who is
wrong.

You could say that the spiritual authority of the head is a
paradox. Mark speaks of this paradox.

Mark 9:35 (NIV)

*"If anyone wants to be first, he must be the very last, and the servant
of all."*

If the husband is to be the first, or the head in the family, he must
be the last. Jesus demonstrated this in His life as an example to us.
He came to serve and not be served (Mark 10:45) and yet
unquestionably has authority (John 13:3&4).

The husband, as the head of the family, gets his spiritual
authority the same way. The head's goal should be to serve the
family and not be served by the family. Jesus had people who

willingly followed Him and served Him. It works the same way in our lives. If we operate in headship as Jesus did, our wife and family will be willing to follow and serve us.

Being the head may not be what you thought it would be. However, if you do it God's way, you will be anointed. I tried it my way, and it did not work. My way, and your way, will fail. Only by doing it God's way will you succeed as the head.

The Wife's Role. Helper? Submitter? Or something more?

There seems to be a lot of controversy regarding the wife's role in the marriage relationship. This is odd since the Bible is very clear on the wife's role. It is found in Genesis.

Genesis 2:18 (AMP)
"Now the Lord God said, It is not good (sufficient, satisfactory) that the man should be alone; I will make him a helper meet (suitable, adapted, complementary) for him."

Here God says he is creating a suitable helper for Adam—one that is adapted to him and whose abilities will be complementary to his.

So the wife's God given role is to be a suitable helper. Suitable means to be precisely adapted to a particular use or purpose, able, and qualified. The wife is all of these things for her husband. Out of the three billion plus women living on earth, God chose your spouse as the perfect wife for you! (That goes for you wives also; out of the three billion men on earth, your husband is the perfect, God chosen, one for you.)

The Submission Thing

Let's face it, a lot of women think submission is a dirty word. This is because we are often wrongly taught that this is the woman's role. It is a responsibility of the role, but as you saw above, that is not the role. Ephesians talks about submission.

Ephesians 5:22 (NKJV)
"Wives, submit to your own husbands, as to the Lord."

Submission in the New Testament is the Greek word "hupotasso" which means to subordinate, be obedient, or to submit yourself to. Webster defines submission as being under one's authority.

Given these scriptures and what we discussed regarding the husband's role above, it is apparent that the husband is the head of the marriage relationship. So what does submission mean exactly? Especially in light of scriptures like Ephesians 5:21 which says we are to "submit to one another" (that "one another" includes husbands and wives).

One way to explain submission is to describe what it is not. Submission does not mean letting your husband have his way and then having a bad attitude about it. Submission involves encouragement, getting on board with the program, no turning back; pushing forward like it was the only decision that could have been made. Submission does not say, "I told you so" if a decision of the head does not work out.

Submission is not hard as long as everyone wants to do the same thing. That's really not even submitting. Submission really only comes in to play when you don't agree or want to do the same thing. But somebody has to be in charge. The husband is the head.

Colossians 3:18 says that wives are to submit to their husband "in the Lord." This means the wife is to submit to the husband's Godly leading. It does not mean the wife is to obey to the point of being led into sin. The Bible says in Romans 13:1 and Titus 3:1 to submit to the authorities and rulers appointed over us; the word used for submit in these scriptures is also the Greek word hupotasso. In Acts 5 Peter and company are preaching the gospel. They get called on the carpet by the council. The Bible says that Peter is supposed to submit to the council since they are the governing authorities. But the council told them to stop preaching in Jesus' name, which is contrary to God's word. Peter and the others told the council the following.

Acts 5:29 (NIV)
"Then Peter and the apostles replied, we must obey God rather than men."

What can we draw from this regarding submission? Simply that a wife must keep God first while submitting to her husband.

If the wife believes her husband's judgment concerning a situation is wrong, she should tell him so. She is, after all, his ideally suited helper. How can she help if she does not offer her assistance to the best of her ability? To let the husband do whatever he thinks best, even if the wife sees potential problems, is not being submissive, it is being foolish.

If the pilot of a plane makes a mistake, the co-pilot is there to make a correction and help avoid a serious accident. The role of the wife is similar. Husbands, there is only one person in the world who is anointed and equipped by God as your helper and who is precisely adapted to your particular situation, need or circumstance, and that person is your wife. You would be a fool to not to listen, and lend great weight, to the advice and guidance of your wife. No man is an island; even the President of the United States has a host of appointees and advisors to help him. But the final decision does rest with the husband.

Reverence your Husband

Finally, we find in Ephesians that the wife is to reverence her husband. The Amplified Bible really brings out the meaning in this scripture.

Ephesians 5:33 (AMP)
"...Let the wife see that she respects and reverences her husband [that she notices him, regards him, honors him, prefers him, venerates, and esteems him; and that she defers to him, praises him, and loves and admires him exceedingly]."

This doesn't need a whole lot of explanation, but putting it into practice will likely bring you closer to your husband than you were before. Reverencing your husband does not mean putting him ahead of God or making him into an idol. It simply means to respect and honor him. For example, value his opinion above others. Go to him for his opinion. Prefer him above other people. For example, when you get a new hairdo, whose opinion do you value most, your husband's or someone else's? You should value your husband's opinion more. Defer to him.

Different Roles—Perfect Fit

Both the husband and wife need to recognize and accept that God has ordained different roles for them. Accept His wisdom in the matter and receive the anointing and blessings that come from working with His plan instead of against it. God has equipped and anointed you to fulfill your role. You are not equipped or anointed to fulfill the role of your spouse. One role is not better than the other, they are just different. Husbands and wives need to value and rely on one another. Usually in a marriage you find that in areas where one spouse is weak the other may be strong and vice versa. Therefore, the husband and wife separately are incomplete, but together they are whole or one. Recognition of this fact, and identification of each spouse's strengths, helps make the marriage relationship work together in a complimentary way.

The marriage and family work best when each person goes all out to fulfill their role and avoids trying to make up for what you may think are your spouse's deficiencies. You wouldn't try to fly a bicycle off a cliff or sit under a chair instead of on it. Both a bicycle and a chair work best when used in their correct role. In the same way, when the husband and wife fulfill their roles the marriage works better.

Chapter 8

THE STORY OF US —
OUR TESTIMONY

OUR marriage counselor, a PhD psychologist, had called my wife Rebekah in for a one-on-one session. "Sit down Rebekah," she said. Rebekah was curious. Our counselor had never asked to meet with one of us alone before. She wasn't prepared for what she was about to hear.

"In my 15 years of marriage counseling, I have never told anyone this before, but you need to get a divorce. Your marriage is hopeless. In fact, I think your husband has the personality type of a serial killer. There's no telling what he could do. I recommend you take what you can get and leave soon. Don't say a word to him—just leave! Here's my home phone number in case you can't get out in time."

Rebekah was stunned. She didn't know what to say. Suddenly it appeared that not only was her marriage over, but she and the kids might even be in danger.

Believe it or not, this was a turning point—for the better—in our marriage. This event happened in early 1991. Rebekah and I are now happily married and helping others save and strengthen their marriages.

This chapter gives our testimony. We don't give our testimony just to talk about the awful things we went through. We tell it

to show that we can relate to the marriage problems you may be
having, to show that you're not the only one with problems, and to
show you that there really is hope for you.

Many people have experienced problems similar to ours.
Often, when people are in the middle of a bad marriage, they
feel like they are the only person in the world experiencing the
problems that they are going through. I know because I used to feel
that way. I'd think to myself, "Nobody else in the world has to put up
with this!"

Most people think their situation is really different than anyone
else's. They think if anyone finds out what's going on, people will
think they are messed up and they won't be accepted; people won't
want to have anything to do with you. They are afraid of rejection and
embarrassment. Maybe you feel this way. Be assured that you are not
the only one who has had problems in marriage, and your problems
aren't even unique. No matter how bad and how hopeless you think
your marriage may be, or how unusual you think your problems are,
we have been there. If we made it through what happened to us and
God is using us to help others, then there is hope for you. You can
have the marriage you've always dreamed of—with your current
spouse!

Rebekah and I met in the late 1980s when I was working as a
civil service employee for the Air Force. At this point in our lives,
neither Rebekah nor I were Christians. In fact, I was an atheist. I
had decided that God wasn't real. Basically, an atheist becomes the
God of their own life. The only standard of right and wrong is what
they think is right and wrong.

Rebekah was a sergeant in the Air Force. She had a very
promising career as a computer systems specialist. She was part of a
team that traveled all over the country setting up new computer systems
at various Air Force bases. This was a prestigious position and she had
been successful in her career.

When we met, she had been divorced about a year. She and her
two small children had just been reassigned to the same base

where I worked. Rebekah's mother, Sandi, was my co-worker. Since Rebekah was available and had sworn marriage off forever, her mother thought it would be a good idea to fix her up with somebody to help her forget the divorce and get on with life. The best choice, she reasoned, would be someone who would not get too serious. I was the "confirmed bachelor" in the office. Most folks thought I would never marry. Since I was not the "marrying type," Sandi decided I was the perfect person to date Rebekah. So, she introduced us.

One of the first things Rebekah told me was that she had no interest in ever getting married again. That was fine with me. I was working on a Master's degree, which only left free time for us to date on Saturday evenings. This suited her perfectly since it gave her plenty of time for her children and to do the other things she wanted.

Several months later I completed my Master's degree and decided that in order to get where I wanted to go in my career, I was going to have to leave civil service and go to work in the commercial world. I started sending out resumes and interviewing. It wasn't very long before I was offered a job by a large firm located about two hours away by car. I accepted the job.

There was one small catch with moving two hours away. I had fallen in love with Rebekah and she with me. After giving it some thought, I decided that I did not want to leave her behind. So one afternoon when we were driving into town in my Toyota Celica, I proposed to her (As you can imagine, it was a very romantic setting!). She accepted even though she felt very good about where she was in her life. She owned a house and had a secure job and a bright future. Accepting my offer of marriage meant giving that up since she would have to move with me. But she felt like she could trust me since we had grown very close. She thought I wanted the same kind of life she did. We were both naïve. We assumed that we each had the same perception of what marriage ought to be.

We should have gotten a big clue when I bought a house in the town that would become our new home. I knew how much money I wanted to spend, and found a house that I liked and that was in my budget. It was a small A-frame; I liked its rustic, woodsy feel. Rebekah, however, hated it; it was smaller than her current home and the lot was wooded. I thought she was just being a crybaby. After all, it had three bedrooms, one for us and one for each of the kids. That was the only requirement that mattered —to me anyway! I just figured she would get over it and see it my way. I didn't know what the big deal was. After all, it was my house, why should she have any input?

I purchased the house and moved away to begin my new job. After I moved, our relationship changed. At least from Rebekah's perspective it did—everything seemed great to me. She felt that overnight I had become a different person. For example, she came to visit a couple of weeks after I moved. She says she felt like an annoying relative who just showed up on the doorstep unannounced to spend the night. This worried her. She thought I was not altogether glad to see her—that maybe my new job had become the "new love" in my life. She pushed the thought out of her head, writing it off as an adjusting period I was going through. She figured that once she moved in, everything would get back to normal.

A couple of months later, Rebekah gave up her career and was discharged from the Air Force. She rented out her house and moved in with me. We didn't get married right away. You see, I thought it would be a good idea to live together for a while until we got married. In my mind, it was no big deal. Marriage was just a formality. We could always make it official later. No need to rush! I simply didn't see where marriage was any better than living together. To me one was as good as the other. This attitude made Rebekah nervous. Alarms were starting to sound! This was not according to the original plan. She suddenly realized she was stuck in a bad situation. She had given everything up. There was no going back to her old job in the military. She had no job, no money, and was living with someone who was in no hurry to get married. All she could do was hope things changed.

Things did not get back to normal. In fact, our relationship began to erode. Several circumstances played a role in that. One, of course, was our not marrying. We lived together for about six months. Let me say one thing about living together; living together and expecting to have a successful relationship is like jumping off a cliff and expecting to find a parachute on the way down. Both are bad decisions and will end in disaster unless a miracle happens.

Secondly, when we both lived in our previous town, I worked at a job I felt I had conquered—a job that I intended to leave. That job was not important to me. I still wanted to do well at it, but it was not my focus. Since I had no job to focus on, I had focused my attention on wooing Rebekah. However, now I had a new career to conquer and it quickly became the focus of my attention; Rebekah was no longer the center of my life.

Finally, in our previous town, we both worked and maintained separate households. She had her money and I had mine. Rebekah was used to relying on herself for money. She could budget and spend her money as she wanted. I too was used to just taking care of me financially. Suddenly we were both thrust into a new situation. Rebekah had to rely on me for support, and I was taking care of a family on my income alone. I was absolutely clueless as to what it really cost to support a family. Not only that, but I was also clueless about the responsibility of caring for a family and managing a household. Rebekah had tried to talk to me about this, starting with the house, but I would not listen to her. These circumstances caused a great amount of stress, frustration, and offense in our already shaky relationship.

So here we were, living together in a strange town. Rebekah found that she was no longer number one. In fact, she thought I was beginning to resent her and the kids. Because of the increased expenses, I was encouraging her to get a job. She now tells me that I really made her feel like I wanted to maintain separate incomes just like before we lived together. I am sure I gave that impression, since she had no money. When we needed groceries, I would go to the store, pick out what I wanted, and buy them. She would ask for things like milk and bread. But I never gave her any money and let her do the shopping. I also hid my credit cards from her. When she asked why I put them in a basket on the top of the refrigerator, I told her, "I've been told never to trust a woman with your money". Rebekah had never done anything to make me suspicious. She had never taken money or credit cards of mine. I was just determined to do things my way. I was very selfish and self-centered. So I see now why she thought the way she did.

As for me, I had the pressure of a new job, financial pressure I had never experienced or expected, and responsibility for a family that I had no idea how to handle. Also, I really wasn't committed to her as shown by me not wanting to get married. To top it all off, all of these problems were squeezed into that little A-frame house with us.

I hope that you can see that the circumstances we were living in did not lend themselves to a harmonious relationship. And believe me, we didn't see much harmony! We argued a lot, but Rebekah could argue like no woman I'd ever seen, and she could throw things with crashing, pinpoint accuracy. The question isn't whether our neighbors heard us. No doubt they did. The question is, why didn't they call the police? I still haven't figured that one out.

As dumb as it may sound, I thought that having a family would not really change my lifestyle very much. You see, I expected I would still be able to do whatever I wanted. I behaved very much like this and was completely surprised when Rebekah expected me to be any different. There is one example of this that really sticks out in my mind. I finished my bachelor's degree when I was still in the Air Force living in the dormitories. Since the dorms were very noisy, I got into the habit of wearing earplugs in the evenings to help drown out the noise when I studied. I really got used to that, and when I completed my degree, I would still wear earplugs at night when I would read, and I liked to read a lot. In fact, I used to have a problem with insomnia, and reading with earplugs became part of my nightly ritual to help me unwind so I could sleep. This habit carried over to when Rebekah and I began living together. Around seven-thirty each evening, I would start reading—with the earplugs in—until going to bed. I know this sounds ridiculous, but it is true. Here I was reading on the couch with these earplugs in and Rebekah and the kids were doing the after dinner things like taking baths, getting ready for the next day, or bed, or whatever. At the time, wearing the earplugs seemed to me like a perfectly reasonable thing to do. It helped me deal with insomnia. Rebekah interpreted the meaning as something very different. She thought I was very blatantly making my own space by cutting her and the kids out of my evenings and my life. I told her nothing to make her feel otherwise.

My expectation that my life would not really change was a far cry from reality. I suppose I thought living with Rebekah would be more like a roommate situation. I thought she would be part of my career and support me in conquering it. I expected her to understand that my career had to take a high priority because it was our livelihood and that we all would have to make sacrifices for me to succeed. My expectations were wrong.

Rebekah, on the other hand, was also finding that reality was vastly different from her expectations. She thought I would be just like I was during the "wooing stage;" someone who loved her and put her first; whose world revolved around her and the family. Her expectations were not being met. In fact, she was looking for the door.

Believe me; my description of this is very tame. The words on the pages cannot convey the strife that we were experiencing. We fought a lot. Daily. Home life was horrible for both of us. My new job was going well, however. To try to compensate for the problems at home, I began focusing more and more attention on my job and less and less on Rebekah (if this was possible). My new employer liked me and there seemed to be opportunity for advancement. I really liked the "attaboys" I was getting from my job. My mind was constantly seeking ways to further advance my career. I decided I needed to get a professional certification to really establish my expertise at work and set me apart from the crowd. I began a four-month process of studying for the examination. More earplugs. More nose in the books. Less time for Rebekah and the kids. I passed the exam, but more damage was done to our relationship. As far as Rebekah was concerned, my job was her direct competitor and she despised it.

One day, during the time that we were living together, Rebekah told me that she was pregnant. I couldn't believe it. Here we were already under financial stress, our relationship was terrible, and a baby was on the way. I asked Rebekah to get an abortion; actually I pretty much insisted. This is horrible, but I believed the propaganda I'd heard about an unborn fetus not being a person. I really believed it was just a mass of tissue that became a baby sometime during the nine-month gestation period. Therefore, I saw nothing wrong with abortion. Rebekah agreed to do it. At the time, I had the impression that she was a willing participant. However, she later told me that she agreed to it because she thought I'd leave her and the kids and they would be on the street if she didn't get the abortion.

I had not proven to be her dreams come true, but I was the means of support for her and the kids. She felt trapped; she had given up her career in the Air Force and had nowhere to go and no way to support herself. She had her house rented, but it was just covering the mortgage. She had a lot of experience with computers but she had never completed a college degree. Thus, she found it very difficult to find a job making enough money to support her and the children. So here she was feeling trapped and unwanted. She felt there was no hope of things getting better and that her only option was to go along with the abortion. One morning I drove

Rebekah to an abortion clinic about an hour away, and we had the abortion done. It was several years before I really understood what we had done that day.

Our relationship sank to even greater depths after that. If you've ever wondered what a vicious cycle is, let me describe one to you. Our constant fighting affected the kids. They were always getting sick. We literally took one or the other, and sometimes both, of them to the doctor every week for ear infections or some other illness. The kids were not covered by my insurance, so every doctor visit and medical bill was something else to pay for. This added to our financial difficulties. The constant illnesses and increased financial pressure further eroded our relationship. I saw my job as the only answer to our financial problems, and in hopes of getting a promotion, I became more obsessed with work! Must work hard! Must get promotion! Must make more money!!

I had always been a casual beer drinker, but now I really began to booze it up. I kept a cold one handy. Drink a beer—forget the checkbook!

One day, however, a practical solution to our financial problem occurred to me. If Rebekah and I got married, I could claim her and the kids as tax deductions, which would greatly increase my net income! Plus, I could add them all to my insurance coverage which would further relieve the financial burden of the medical bills. What a genius I was!! Love was not my motive for finally getting married. My motive was to get a tax break and save a buck.

When I told Rebekah that I thought we should go ahead and marry, she was happy at first. But then I explained my thought process to her. Rebekah's dreams were steam rolled. You can imagine how "happy" she was to hear why I wanted to get married. If she thought she was past feeling, this jolt was the icing on the cake. She had hoped that we would have a nice wedding. Even more, she had hoped that my attitude toward her would somehow change, that I would stop thinking of her as a tax break, that I would find in her again what I had before. When she originally decided to marry me, back before she moved in with me, she spent several weeks shopping for a wedding gown. Even though Rebekah had been married before, she had not had a nice wedding with the wedding gown, the multi layered cake, the romantic honeymoon, and all of the other frills that women dream about and expect in such a special event. But I had no appreciation for her dream whatsoever. All I knew was that we could get a tax break. When she asked me when I wanted to get married, I told her, we could do it on my lunch hour. This was a romantic moment rivaled only by my proposal in the Toyota Celica. I really hit this one out of the park.

So, with her wedding gown hanging in the closet, Rebekah and I went to the Justice of the Peace one Saturday morning and got married. (Yep, she talked me out of doing it during my lunch break.) No honeymoon, no cake, nothing. She wanted the whole "wedding" thing. She wanted people there with us when we got married. I said no. She wanted to invite our parents and have them come. I said no. She wanted to call our parents and at least let them know we were getting married. I told her it wasn't a big deal. She called her parents right before we left the house. After we got married, she asked to go out to eat breakfast to celebrate. It was only nine o'clock in the morning when we got married. I knew she wanted all this "stuff", but it was more important for me to be in control. No going out for breakfast that morning. I was not letting her control me, and I certainly didn't want to start things out by letting her think she could do something just because she wanted to. In fact, it was a few weeks later before Rebekah and I made love to consummate the marriage. This was a strange issue and illustrates how hardheaded people can be. You see, I knew she would want to consummate the marriage even though we had obviously been sleeping together for over six months. I knew she thought this was what we were supposed to do—part of the "marriage tradition" thing. I wasn't giving an inch to her. I was in control, besides, it held no special meaning for me. It was one more stake through her heart.

It was not long after this that Rebekah actually began to wonder if I might be the anti-Christ. Just look at it from her perspective. I was obsessed with climbing the corporate ladder and appeared to only want a family to make me look good. She figured a nice looking family would help me make the desirable impression at company picnics and parties. I was also very interested in someday getting involved in politics. All of this equaled "anti-Christ" to her. She asked me about it one day. I told her she wasn't the first person who had asked me this. I thought it was cool that she thought this. But, you know, it made me wonder. What if I was the anti-Christ and just didn't know it?

Once I could claim Rebekah and the kids as dependents our finances improved a little bit, but not enough to remove the pressure. We still struggled in that area. I began to look for someone or something to blame for this problem. First, I blamed my job for not paying me enough. In this position, I was helping train people who, in some cases, made several thousand dollars a year more than I did. Secondly, I blamed the town we lived in because it was a higher cost of living area than the town I'd left. This led me to conclude that I needed to find a higher paying job in a different location. As an added bonus, I figured that more money and a shot at getting the heck out of that A-frame would make Rebekah happy. Thus, I began sending out resumes and interviewing again.

Rebekah was all for the idea of leaving. After all, it was after we moved here that our relationship went south. It was here that she became the lowest priority in my life. It was here that life was the pits. It was here that she couldn't get a good job of her own. It was here that the kids were constantly sick. She thought, as I did, that leaving would be the answer. She really wanted a fresh start somewhere else.

During the job search, however, we still had to live with our circumstances and ourselves. It continued to be bad. I began to drink more and more. One beer in the evening became two. Two became three. Two or three beers a day became routine. A case bought Friday night seldom lived to see the daylight of Monday morning. It's amazing how you always can find the money to buy stuff like that. I knew I was drinking a lot. I also knew that it could become a problem. Every once in a while, I would take a few days off from drinking. I did it to just be certain I was still in control and not the bottle.

Our relationship was so bad that Rebekah thought I tried to kill her one time. She got really bad heartburn high up in her throat. She said it felt like she had swallowed jagged glass. Finally she decided that I must have poisoned her. Our relationship was so bad that she thought I would actually kill her to end it. She asked me, "What did you poison me with? At least tell me that before I die?" I did not try to kill her, but I was so cold hearted she thought that I would.

Then we got pregnant again. We were amazingly careless about using contraception. Although we were married, Rebekah had just gotten a decent job, not great, but better by far than her previous job prospects. I had been telling her that a job would help build her self-esteem, confidence, feelings of worth, and so on. I felt that way, didn't everyone? Besides, I figured that if she just stayed home with the kids, her brain would turn to mush (I think just the opposite about stay-at-home moms now!). When she became pregnant the second time, I was not supportive—not in her eyes. When she asked me what I wanted her to do, I told her, "Whatever you want to do." I thought I was being supportive of whatever decision she made, but she did not take my response that way. She thought I wanted her to have another abortion.

Early in the pregnancy, she started having complications. Probably stress had a lot to do with it. Her doctor told her she needed to stay on bed rest or she could lose the baby. Of course going to bed meant she would lose her new job. When she asked what I thought, I gave her my supportive, "Do whatever you want to." As I said, she took that to mean that I was not happy about the baby or the potential loss of her job.

After about a month Rebekah had a miscarriage, or so she told me at the time. I later learned that because of all the pressure she felt from me, she had gotten another abortion. She was afraid that I would ultimately leave her if we had the baby.

After the "miscarriage", Rebekah went into a severe depression. She had tremendous feelings of guilt about what she had done and, because she'd done it in secret, she bore these feelings all alone. It was a horrible time. Going out of the house terrified her. She hated to see pregnant women or women with infant children. She began to drink a lot; white Russians I think it was. I knew something really bad was going on when she asked me if I'd take care of the kids if something bad happened to her. She had become suicidal.

Early one morning, around 2:00 AM, she tried to kill herself. I had drunk my usual and gone to sleep like usual. I don't know why I woke up, but suddenly I did. It's an odd thing when someone half-drunk wakes up from a dead sleep. That just doesn't happen. I think God woke me up that night. Anyway, I woke up and noticed the light was still on in the living room. I got up and went to see why the light was on so late. Rebekah was sitting on the sofa, cutting her wrists with a razor blade. I had to physically take the razor blade away from her to stop her. I called 911. Rebekah didn't want me to call them; she wanted to finish the job. She wanted nothing to do with paramedics trying to save her. She took off running out of the house and down the street. I had to chase her down. There she was sprinting down the driveway and the street, with me, still partly toasted and bare footed, chasing her. Let me tell you, that girl was fast. I only caught her because she stumbled and fell down. I leaped on her, and physically drug her back to the house. It wasn't easy. She didn't want to go. I had to sit on her until the paramedics arrived. Had I not woken up, I am sure Rebekah would be dead now.

The paramedics finally arrived, asked some questions that I

don't remember, and took Rebekah to the emergency room. At that moment, I didn't care. Not one bit. I did not intend to go see how she was. I figured that was it, good riddance, it's over now, I will never see her again as long as I live. Just give me a divorce and let's call this thing quits.

Then I found a suicide note that Rebekah had written. The note was lost long ago, and I don't remember exactly what it said. I do recall this. She apologized for what had happened with us, for how bad life had become. She said she loved me and that she wished I loved her. She asked me to make sure the kids were taken care of. After reading the note and thinking for a few minutes, my heart went out to Rebekah. Way down deep under all the ugliness and hurt, hidden in a dark corner, I realized that I still had love for her. I could not communicate or show my love in a way that she could understand, but I did still love her. Suddenly I realized that I couldn't leave her in that state of mind, all alone and afraid, in a hospital full of strangers. I woke up the kids and we all went to the hospital. I brought Rebekah home a little later that day.

It didn't end there. It was several weeks, maybe longer, before she was out of the woods with the potential for suicide. I sincerely hope you never experience what we went through during this time. The drive to commit suicide has to be a demonic thing. Rebekah used to have vivid nightmares in which someone named Isaac urged her to kill herself. A couple of times at night I would wake up to find Rebekah sleep walking in search of razor blades. I had hidden all of the razor blades in the house where she couldn't find them. One night however, she woke me up sleepwalking; I sat up in bed and watched her go straight to where I had hidden the razor blades. I stopped her of course and woke her up. She said that someone in her nightmare told her where to find them.

Sometimes she would be having horrible nightmares and couldn't wake up. I would have to shake her and shake her for several minutes to wake her up. Other times at night, I would listen to make sure she was still breathing. I was concerned that she might try to overdose on pills or something. I stayed awake all night many times watching to make sure she didn't kill herself. Finally, I got so exhausted that one night I started tying her ankle to mine with a rope so I could sleep, knowing that if she got out of bed the tug would wake me up. This went on for many days. As I said, it was a horrible time for both of us.

Finally, after what seemed like a very long time, she began to come out of it. Our lives took on some normalcy, or at least what was normal for us. Then, one night we went out drinking together and got into a physical fight. It was the only time we ever did that. Rebekah scratched my face and left five or six long, bloody scratches on it. I literally thought she was trying to scratch out my eyes, so I struck her to make her stop and hit her in the nose. The blow broke her nose and gave her two black eyes. For several weeks, we both had physical, as well as emotional scars, as a constant, visible reminder of what had happened.

Not long after this incident I landed a job with another company that paid me 28% more and moved us to a town on the Mississippi Gulf Coast. We rented out our current house and bought a big, roomy house less than a block from the beach. Things were looking up!

For a couple of months, things were better between Rebekah and me. I think the change of scenery, larger home, and better finances, distracted us for a while. It gave me a false sense that our troubles were over, and I began to think we could really be happy together. Soon the newness of everything wore off, and we were still there with the same old problems. With the exception of the severe financial problems, our relationship returned to horrible status.

My drinking continued to increase. I'd gotten to the point that I would drink a six-pack of beer every evening and more than a case on the weekends. I knew this was not good, so one day I decided to take my usual break from drinking to make sure I hadn't become an alcoholic. But this time I'd gone too long. The very first night the craving for a beer was so bad that I couldn't stand it. I had to go and buy some. This literally scared the heck out of me. I was no longer in control; the alcohol was in control, and I knew it. I had become an alcoholic. I did not tell Rebekah although I am sure I did not have to. She could see it for herself. Sometimes, she would come home and there I would be, beer in hand, having my own private party. She knew I had a problem.

To help her cope with our problems, Rebekah tried smoking marijuana a few times. She had smoked it in high school and enjoyed it then. So she reasoned it would give her an escape from her current problems. She thought it would take away the emotional pain, at least for a little while. This time, however, it wasn't enjoyable and it didn't take away the pain. The pain never went away no matter how high she got. She was looking to the pot to find an escape from the pain of rejection, guilt, and all of the other problems. It didn't work, so she quit.

Our fighting was as bad as ever. Finally, our communications came to a dead halt. We couldn't talk about anything. All we did was argue. If one of us tried to say something the other assumed the worst was coming, went on the defensive, and a major brawl would erupt. I began trying to avoid even talking to her, or being in the same room with her.

Finally, Rebekah asked me if I would go to marriage counseling with her. I didn't really want to because I didn't think our relationship was worth saving. I agreed to go basically so no one could say I didn't try to save our marriage. I was more concerned about what people would think than about our marriage. We checked around and found the most reputable counselor in the area. This brings us back to the beginning of this chapter. We met with the counselor several times, and that one occasion she asked to meet with Rebekah alone.

When Rebekah came home from the one-on-one session, I knew something was up. Rebekah was acting really strange toward me. She would look at me all big eyed, and when I'd ask her what was going on she'd say, "Nothing. Everything's fine. Nothing's wrong." Of course, what the counselor told her had her shaken up.

I finally got Rebekah to tell me what was wrong. That's when she told me that the counselor told her we were hopeless, we should get divorced, and I was a Jekyll and Hyde type capable of who knows what. I got a good laugh out of it. I thought it was ridiculous that the counselor thought I was like that. But it had really hit home with Rebekah. It confirmed all of the thoughts Rebekah had about me. She thought I was trying to kill her on more than one occasion, and someone else had seen how cold I could be.

However, the counselor's statement that we were hopeless - the only hopeless case she had ever seen - and that we should get a divorce, was the final nail in the coffin. It was over. We had come to the end of ourselves and found that divorce was the only answer. Even friends whom we had confided in advised us to get divorced. Rebekah and I talked about it. I wanted a divorce. Rebekah didn't, but she would not stand in the way. I said earlier that this event was a turning point for the good in our relationship. The reason this was a good thing is because this is when we admitted we could do nothing to save our relationship; an outside force would have to lend a hand if anything was to be done.

The decision to get a divorce hurt Rebekah horribly. She agreed to it without a fight because she did not want to give me the satisfaction of knowing how hurt she was by it.

She began looking for a job so she would be financially on her feet when the divorce was final. She wanted to get as far away as possible. One night, looking at the want ads in the paper, she found out about some job openings in Australia (of all places). She must have really wanted to get as far away from me as possible, because she sent them her resume. They actually called her a couple of times and told her she was a leading candidate for one of the jobs. All the while, Rebekah felt like her life was over. She loved me in spite of all the bad times—more than she cared to admit. She figured Australia would force her to get over me because of the great distance. Because she loved me very much, she felt it would be too painful to live anywhere close. Australia made perfect sense to her.

She knew she had to manage in the meantime. She had come to the end of herself, so she returned to her roots. Rebekah had grown up in church and believed God was real. Even though her experience was small, she thought maybe God could help her. She started going to churches to try to find someone who knew something about God. She went and talked to one pastor about her problems. He held out no hope for her whatsoever. He said that eventually she'd get over the divorce and get on with life. At another church, they told her the pastor wouldn't be able to talk to her for a few weeks. Then she stumbled upon the pastor of a small, non-denominational church. Rebekah told him about her problems and stunningly he told her, "Rebekah, God does not want you to get a divorce, and He does not want to give you a new husband. He wants to save the husband you have." Rebekah was amazed to hear this. She was so used to hopelessness that for someone to hold out hope was shocking. The other churches made her feel that God was powerless to help her. This pastor boldly said that God wanted to help and could help. He was the only person who had ever offered Rebekah any hope that our marriage could be saved.

Rebekah became a Christian, and she and the kids began attending this church regularly. She began witnessing to me and even had the pastor come over and talk to me. Oddly enough, in my heathen state I actually liked this guy. I like him so much that I offered him a beer during a visit. Rebekah asked me not to do that again in the future.

Rebekah got very involved in this church and all she would talk about was Jesus. I started thinking she'd gone off the deep end. As I said earlier, I was an atheist.

We went on for several weeks this way—Rebekah witnessing to me and me thinking she was nuts. I remember a few nights sitting on the front porch thinking the mosquitoes would keep her in the house so she wouldn't witness to me. But no—there she was going on and on.

Our relationship was still bad. Although Rebekah did not want a divorce, living in this bad relationship was quickly becoming intolerable. It was very painful to stay there while being rejected by me. She and a lot of other people at the church were praying for me.

It wasn't long before Rebekah had had it up to her ears with the situation. She was believing God for a miracle. She was continually praying and asking God that I would either leave her and He would take the pain away, or that I would get born again and change. She couldn't take it much longer.

Then late one evening we were sitting on the front porch together. Rebekah was witnessing to me as usual. Suddenly, amazingly, she heard a voice say, "In one week everything will be OK." She looked at me and said, "Did you hear anything." I hadn't heard a thing and she didn't tell me what she had heard. Rebekah saw the pastor the next day. She told him what had happened and that she thought she was either going crazy or God had spoken to her. He reassured her that she was not crazy. He said something very wise to her. He said, "If I had called you two months ago, you would not have recognized my voice because you didn't know who I was then." He told her, "If God did speak to you; you probably would not recognize His voice either, because you haven't gotten to know Him yet." He told her he wasn't sure if she had heard God, and that she would just have to wait and see what happened to find out if it was God.

A couple of days later, Rebekah was praying and she had a vision. She saw me lying in a hospital bed in a coma. She was sitting in a chair by the bed and a doctor was standing by the door shaking his head as if to say, "There's nothing more that we can do." Then Rebekah told me about the vision and what she had heard. She told me I had better be sure to wear my seat belt and drive carefully. She told me, "I think God might kill you". I discounted it entirely. I figured this was confirmation that she was nuts. Rebekah thought the vision meant that God was going to kill me. She reasoned in her mind that if I died she would eventually get over it, much easier than getting over the divorce. But that was not what it meant. She told the pastor about the vision. After considering for a few minutes, he told her that it probably wasn't a physical deathbed, but a spiritual one. He said it was up to me.

A few days later, Rebekah had another vision. She saw the hospital bed that she had seen earlier, only this time, I wasn't in it. The bed was empty. This really scared her; she thought that surely it meant I was going to die. She even told me that she thought God was going to kill me, and explained what she saw.

Later that night there was a special late night prayer meeting at her church. She went and while there talked to someone about her vision and asked them what they thought it might mean. This person said they thought it meant I was in God's hands. That made her feel better, but she still didn't understand.

I was highly concerned about Rebekah going to this late night prayer meeting. A motorcycle gang was having some sort of convention in the area. The prayer meeting ran very late and I had a lot of time to myself to think. As I said earlier, I still loved Rebekah, but I simply could not express my love to her or even get along with her for that matter. When it got really late and Rebekah still wasn't home I began to think, "What if the bikers got her!" (There were no cell phones then.) I could just imagine the car breaking down and this biker gang coming along. The more I thought about it, the more I became convinced that was what had happened. I got worried and decided that if God was real He could take care of her. Right there I decided that it was time to accept Jesus Christ. It was about 11:30 PM and it was exactly one week from when Rebekah had heard His voice on the front porch; His voice that said everything would be OK in one week. You know, that fact didn't occur to me that I was accepting Christ exactly one week from the day Rebekah had heard His voice. If I had thought about that, I probably wouldn't have accepted Jesus that night, just to spite Rebekah and make sure she was wrong. Anyway, that's when I became a Christian. I believe the pastor was right about Rebekah's vision. I was on a spiritual deathbed and the time left for me to get born again and live spiritually was about to run out. Thankfully, I accepted Him. Our journey back had begun.

I need to add one other thing here. Right before I got born again, Rebekah made a deal with me that got me to go to church with her. I wanted her to go to an office party with me. I didn't want anyone at work to know I was having trouble at home. It was a beer party. The deal was that she would go to the party with me if I would go to church with her. She went to the party and I went to church. Something happened at church that day. I saw something I had never seen before. I can't explain it any better than to say that I could see the love that those church people had for each other. I knew in my logical mind that either they were faking it or it was real. I also knew, logically, that there was no way that many people could fake it. Someone would goof it up – it couldn't be a fake. I knew right then that God was real; I left with no doubts. Atheism can't stand up to love. Once you know that God is real, your options become very limited. You only have two; you can accept Him or you can reject Him. Only a fool rejects God when they know He is real. It was a few days later when that late night prayer meeting was taking place. It was that Friday night I gave my life to Jesus. Thank God I wasn't a fool.

Immediately after my salvation, a miracle happened. I no longer had any craving whatsoever for alcohol. As I mentioned earlier, I had drank so much for so long, that I had gotten to the point where I had to drink every day. However, from the moment I was saved, the alcoholism disappeared and the craving has never returned. It was as if God was proving to me that he was real. I knew without a doubt there was no other explanation.

I did not immediately tell Rebekah what had happened. I was just too hardheaded I guess. She knew something had changed though; because I wasn't drinking and I wasn't treating her like "road kill" anymore.

The following Sunday I went to church with her and during the break between Sunday School and Worship Service I told her that I'd gotten born again. She was amazed, of course. I really wanted to keep it low key and didn't want to make a big deal out of it. So, Rebekah told the Pastor. At the beginning of the service, he announced it to the entire church. So much for low key.

From that point on our lives began to change. We had a new commitment to our marriage and a chance to rebuild. I wish I could say that restoring our marriage was easy and quick, but it wasn't. We had to do a lot of work. In fact, at times it was downright hard and slow. There was a whole lot of hurt, pain, guilt and anger in our pasts to deal with. But for the first time ever, we were healing rather than becoming more wounded.

Several months after I got born again, I asked Rebekah if she would like to re-say our wedding vows in the church. She was surprised that I came up with this idea because it was a desire of her heart. We talked to the Pastor and he also thought it was a good idea. As it turned out, the church gave us the "big wedding" Rebekah had always wanted complete with a big wedding cake and a reception. She got to wear the wedding dress she had bought all those years before. We even went away on a honeymoon.

Over the next few years, we worked at restoring our relationship. I must confess that Rebekah was more diligent about it than I was. At times I was a half-hearted participant. It was hard work.

Rebekah and I both got involved in helping out in church. I always wondered specifically what God wanted us to do for Him. One morning I was praying and I asked God what it was that He wanted us to do. God spoke very clearly to me and said,

"Marriages." I was surprised. I had never considered that God might want us, with the horrible marriage history we had, to minister to others on marriage. I went and told Rebekah that God had told me what He wanted us to do for Him, but I refused to tell her what He said. I asked her to pray and see what God told her. I wanted confirmation that this was really God's call on our lives and not just my imagination (although I am certain I never would have imagined He would want us to be involved in Marriage Ministry). Rebekah prayed and a few days later came to me and said, "I feel like God wants us to minister healing to marriages." That was enough for me.

I suppose the bottom line to our testimony is this, where the wisdom of man failed (i.e., the counselor who recommended we get a divorce) God prevailed. God led Rebekah and I full circle, from probably one of the worst marriages you could possibly imagine to one out of which we now are able to minister to others. We found that God had a plan to heal our relationship. Through much prayer, study, and experience, God revealed His plan to us. This book is written to reveal that plan to you.

That's our testimony—at least it's most of it. There are other things that I didn't go into here. Like I tell other people, if I told you everything that happened, you would think I was lying. Hopefully you can get a clear picture that things were not good with us, but that God is a big God.

For both of us, when we talk about what our lives were like back then, it's like we are talking about something that happened to someone else or like something that happened in a movie we saw. That just isn't us anymore. I can honestly say, though, that it was worth it. I wouldn't wish what happened to us on anyone, but if it meant our relationship, I wouldn't even have to think about it. I would do it all again, and more, for Rebekah.

EPILOGUE

Read This Last

I (Rick) lost some weight a few years ago by sticking to a diet plan for several months. I got down to the lowest weight I'd been at in nearly 15 years. That was great. Losing weight is almost always a good thing (for me at least). But a couple of years passed, and I began going back to my old eating habits. I stopped doing the diet plan and gradually began to gain weight again. Over about two years, I gained back half of the weight I had originally lost. Did the plan stop working? No. I stopped working the plan. Do I need to find a new diet? No. I just need to go back and start doing the diet that worked before again. And this time I need to stick with it for the long haul.

Why do I tell this story? Read James to find out.

James 1:23 – 25 (NKJV)
"For if anyone is a hearer of the word and not a doer, he is like a man observing his natural face in a mirror; for he observes himself, goes away, and immediately forgets what kind of man he was. But he who looks into the perfect law of liberty and continues in it, and is not a forgetful hearer but a doer of the work, this one will be blessed in what he does."

After losing all that weight, I did exactly what this scripture is talking. I walked away, forgot what it took to succeed at weight loss, didn't continue in it, and I gained some of the weight back. If I follow the plan, and stick with it, I will succeed.

This book tells you how to have good marriage relationship. The principals of this book apply to all relationships. Reading it and putting it on the shelf won't help though. You need to put the lessons in this book to work in your relationship and stick with it. Don't be like the guy who looked in the mirror, walked away, and forgot what he looked like. Remember to keep doing what works. If it stops working, it isn't because the plan failed; it is because you failed to do the plan.

In the 1960s, the Green Bay Packers were the dominant football team. They were coached by Vince Lombardi. In one game, they were getting beaten badly in the first half. At half time, Coach Lombardi stood in front of the players in the locker room, held up a football, and said, "Gentlemen, this is a football." What was he doing? He was reminding them to stick with the basics. Doing the basics right will result in success. This book teaches the basic truths of what it takes to have good relationship. Stick with them and you will do well.

If you do the right thing long enough, it will work. If you keep doing the right thing, it will keep working. If you stop, you will find yourself back in the same old mess, or maybe in a worse one. This truth is illustrated by Galatians.

Galatians 6:7 – 10 (MSG)

"Don't be misled: No one makes a fool of God. What a person plants, he will harvest. The person who plants selfishness, ignoring the needs of others--ignoring God!- harvests a crop of weeds. All he'll have to show for his life is weeds! But the one who plants in response to God, letting God's Spirit do the growth work in him, harvests a crop of real life, eternal life. So let's not allow ourselves to get fatigued doing good. At the right time we will harvest a good crop if we don't give

up, or quit. Right now, therefore, every time we get the chance, let us work for the benefit of all, starting with the people closest to us in the community of faith."

Your spouse is pretty close to you. Get busy.

Rick and Rebekah

Made in the USA
Middletown, DE
30 March 2021